Fishes and plants in perfect harmony

A FISHKEEPER'S GUIDE TO
MAINTAINING A
HEALTHY AQUARIUM

Trichogaster leeri (*Pearl Gourami*)

A well-balanced freshwater tropical aquarium

A FISHKEEPER'S GUIDE TO
MAINTAINING A
HEALTHY AQUARIUM

Essential advice on all aspects of aquarium care

Dr Neville Carrington

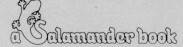

a Salamander book

Published by Salamander Books Limited
LONDON

A Salamander Book

ISBN 86101 235 6

Distributed in the UK by Hodder and Stoughton Services,
P.O. Box 6, Mill Road, Dunton Green, Sevenoaks, Kent TN13 2XX.

Shoaling Characins in ideal surroundings

Credits

Editor: Geoff Rogers
Designer: Tony Dominy
Colour reproductions:
Rodney Howe Ltd.
Filmset: SX Composing Ltd.
Printed in Belgium by Henri Proost & Cie, Turnhout.

Author

Dr. Neville Carrington, an acknowledged innovator in the design of aquarium hardware, has turned his attention to one of his abiding passions – the pursuit of the healthy aquarium. Such a pursuit has led him along many avenues, from tank design to the complex subject of water chemistry. Dr. Carrington's training and experience stand him in good stead for such an investigation. He devised an internationally known liquid food for young fishes while studying for a pharmacy degree and after obtaining a doctorate in Pharmaceutical Engineering Science and a period in industry, he now runs a company developing equipment and chemical products for the aquarium world.

Consultant

Peter W. Scott, MSc., BVSc., MRCVS., MIBiol., is a veterinarian who qualified at Liverpool University with a special interest in fish, reptiles and amphibians. As a member of the International Zoo Veterinary Group, a practice which works solely with zoo and aquatic animals, he is widely involved with public aquaria, fish farmers, retailers and wholesalers and is the Veterinary Adviser to Ornamental Fish International (OFI). He is the author of two books, and numerous articles on various aspects of fish health, on which he has lectured in a number of countries.

Contents

Water: The Total Environment 10
The water cycle; water sources; water hardness; the pH of water; iron and copper compounds; chlorine and chloramine; ammonia, nitrites and nitrates; osmosis; aeration and filtration.

Growing Healthy Aquarium Plants 40
Plastic and real plants; preparing for plants; treating plants; lighting; new techniques to promote plant growth.

Improving Success with Fishbreeding 48
The influence of aquascaping; selection and prior treatment of fishes; water quality; water temperature; lighting; feeding and aeration; pests and diseases.

Avoiding Diseases and Reducing Stress 58
Buying fishes; stocking the aquarium; design and position of the tank; potential hazards of live foods; pests introduced into the aquarium; looking for disease; humane disposal of fishes; using disease remedies; using common salt; approximate water capacity of aquariums; diagnostic guide.

An A-Z of Common Pests and Diseases 76
A comprehensive survey of more than 30 pests and diseases presented in alphabetical order of common name.

Additional Reading 112

Index 113

Credits 116

Water: The Total Environment

Many fishkeepers enjoy success without any specific knowledge of the finer points of water chemistry or fish diseases; they seem to have an instinctive idea of what suits their fishes best and how to nurture them back to health when illness strikes. But such innate appreciation of how to maintain a healthy aquarium is usually based on many years of practical experience. For the thousands of newcomers that join the fishkeeping fraternity every year eagerness to succeed may be a stronger incentive than patience to learn. And so for them – and also for every fishkeeper, however experienced – this book provides an easy-to-follow blend of basic science, up-to-date technical information and practical advice based on a lifetime of hard-won experience. From such a firm foundation, every reader can chart their own journey of discovery through the continual fascination that fishkeeping has to offer.

This first section addresses the vital subject of water chemistry,

not in abstruse isolation but in practical terms relevant to all aspiring and practised fishkeepers alike. The opening part of the text considers the quality of natural water and leads on to an examination of water hardness, its acidity or alkalinity (pH value), the nitrogenous wastes that build up in aquarium water, and the aeration and filtration systems employed to keep it sweet. Throughout, the emphasis is on learning basic principles in a practical context. All technical terms are explained as they are introduced.

Later sections of the book look at ways of growing healthy aquarium plants, how to achieve success with fishbreeding, ways of avoiding diseases and reducing stress, and how to recognize and tackle a wide range of fish pests and diseases. The book is largely aimed at the freshwater tropical aquarium, the most popular branch of the fishkeeping hobby throughout the world. But marines and coldwater fishes are by no means ignored.

For aquatic life water is a total environment. It is not only a medium for movement but it also acts as a carrier for gases – such as oxygen and carbon dioxide – for mineral salts and other substances vital to the well-being of fishes and plants, and as a reservoir for the disposal of waste. Not surprisingly, natural fresh water never approaches the purity possible under laboratory conditions; its complex blend of micro-organisms, dissolved gases and solids influences a wide range of interrelated, easily measurable parameters such as hardness, pH (acidity or alkalinity), nitrite and nitrate.

In normal circumstances many fishes can tolerate a reasonable variation in their water quality; only when they breed may particular conditions be necessary for success. How does the natural water cycle work? What sources of water are available to fishkeepers?

The water cycle
Water circulates in a never-ending sequence of evaporation and condensation – the so-called water cycle. Evaporation from the oceans, rivers and lakes carries water vapour into the atmosphere where it condenses into clouds of water

droplets. The quality of the water that falls as rain depends not only on how it is precipitated but also on changes that occur as it descends. In a thunderstorm, for example, rain absorbs oxides of nitrogen produced by lightning. Dust particles in the air may also cause condensation. And as the rain droplets fall to earth they absorb oxygen, carbon dioxide and other gases; sulphur dioxide emitted from power stations, for example, produces 'acid rain'.

Once rain reaches the ground, further influences are at work. As water percolates through the layers of topsoil it will become further charged with carbon dioxide from the respiration of plant roots and micro-organisms in humus. Excluding any other contaminants, therefore, rain usually becomes weakly acid due to the reaction shown below.

$$CO_2 + H_2O \rightarrow H_2CO_3$$

Carbon dioxide + water → Carbonic acid

Depending on the terrain, other substances will dissolve in groundwater. Humus and peat in the soil may provide organic substances, for example, and nitrates from farmland fertilizers will readily join the 'aqueous cocktail'. Once the water

The sun's heat evaporates water from land and sea.

Water held as clouds of droplets eventually falls as rain.

Lightning fuses nitrogen and oxygen in the atmosphere

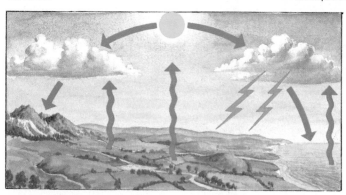

On larval rocks surface water remains very soft.

On pure sand water retains its natural softness.

In chalk or limestone water becomes hard and alkaline.

Water from farmland is rich in organic material.

Underground water is usually hard and high in minerals.

Left: *A tributary of the Itahaem River in Brazil, its soft waters rich in tropical fish species displayed with pride in aquariums throughout the world.*

Above: *The basic elements in the water cycle. The sun provides the energy to initiate the sequence of evaporation and condensation.*

becomes less than pure it actively affects the physical environment around it; the very dilute solution of carbonic acid dissolves minute quantities of calcium carbonate in rocks such as chalk, limestone and dolomite, producing a dilute solution of calcium bicarbonate.

H_2CO_3 +	$CaCO_3$ →	$Ca(HCO_3)_2$
Carbonic acid	Calcium carbonate	Calcium bicarbonate

The bicarbonate produced in the above reaction is unstable and only remains as long as there is an excess of carbonic acid. A similar process occurs with magnesium-bearing rocks (magnesite and dolomite), producing magnesium bicarbonate. Both these bicarbonates give water so-called 'temporary hardness', which is easily removed by boiling, as we shall see later. Any calcium and magnesium carbonates, along with calcium and magnesium sulphates, remaining in the water are the main causes of permanent hardness. The total level of these salts is limited, however, by their low solubility. In comparative terms, calcium sulphate is more soluble than calcium carbonate and will produce a much harder water. Calcium is much more abundant than magnesium in a ratio of 10 parts of calcium to between 1 and 3 parts of magnesium.

Where natural water remains locked underground for many centuries it usually becomes harder as time goes by. The water also dissolves a host of mineral salts, producing spa waters. Although such mineral waters may have therapeutic qualities for man, they are usually unsuitable for aquarium use.

Conversely, if water falls on virtually insoluble larval rock, percolates through pure sand or is essentially surface water, then it will dissolve very few substances and will probably be very soft.

This brief review of the water cycle shows how natural influences affect the final quality of fresh water. Since tapwater is the most accessible supply for most fishkeepers, how does this compare in quality with more natural sources?

Domestic tapwater
Although tapwater is a processed product intended for human consumption, it is usually quite acceptable for aquarium use. Its degree of acidity or alkalinity (pH value) and hardness depend partly on the original source and partly on the treatment given to it. Neutral tapwater is usually treated so that it becomes moderately alkaline – with a pH of 7.5 to 8.0 – which is generally suitable for most fishes and helps to reduce corrosion of water mains. However, most plants grow better as the pH approaches 7.0. The total hardness of tapwater is generally controlled to acceptable limits for fishkeeping. We shall be considering the pH and hardness of water in more detail on pages 16-24

Tapwater usually contains a wide range of substances, including salts of calcium, magnesium and sodium, plus small but vital quantities of trace elements. Levels of copper that are undesirable for fishes may build up in water held in copper pipes for some time, particularly in soft water areas. If possible, test the water for such contaminants and if there is any doubt run plenty to waste before filling the aquarium.

Tapwater is traditionally treated with chlorine to kill harmful micro-organisms. Some domestic water supplies, particularly those with a high

Above: *The dark waters of this Brazilian stream are soft, acidic in nature and full of organic material from rotting vegetation on its banks. Characins abound here.*

organic level (upland 'peat' waters, for example, or those containing organic material leached from farmland or built up through repeated recycling), may be treated with chloramines. This practice causes great concern among fishkeepers, as we shall see on page 25. However, there is now a trend towards using ozone and chlorine dioxide, which minimize the formation of undesirable compounds and produce water that is much more suitable for fishkeeping.

Other additions may include fluoride (to reduce dental decay in children) and water softening chemicals (to discourage scaling of pipes). Your local water authority will be able to supply precise information on the composition of the tapwater.

Although tapwater is suitable for general fishkeeping, later in this section we shall be considering ways of improving its quality for aquarium use. But what of using more natural sources of water, such as rainwater and water from rivers and lakes?

Below: *Water flowing through this limestone cave will become hard from the carbonates, bicarbonates and* *sulphates of calcium and magnesium that dissolve into it from the rock. It will also become alkaline.*

Rainwater

If you are lucky enough to live in an area where the atmosphere is clean, then a rainwater tub is a valuable asset to fishkeeping. Unfortunately, even in apparently clean areas, rainwater can be loaded with contaminants. The dust left by raindrops on a cleanly polished surface indicates how much solid material can be washed out of the atmosphere, even in areas away from industry. It is now clear, for example, that 'acid rain' can fall hundreds of miles away from the original site of pollution. Rainwater can also be contaminated by the surface upon which it falls.

Despite these reservations, however, most rainwater is useful to fishkeepers. Try to avoid using the first rainfall after a dry spell, primarily because it may be more contaminated than succeeding 'batches'. The most practical way of checking its suitability is to keep some fishes in it! If the rainwater passes this test, then it is a cheap and convenient source of soft water. Use it mixed in equal parts with tapwater for a wide range of community fishes, and virtually on its own (and treated with peat) for keeping and breeding Discus, for breeding Neon Tetras, and other selected freshwater fishes.

Natural water sources

The inconvenience involved in collecting natural water, i.e. from rivers and ponds, tends to overshadow its possible usefulness for most fishkeepers. Of course, natural water varies greatly in quality (and also disease potential) depending on its origin, but it may be just the thing to stimulate breeding of a difficult fish or to revive that flagging plant in the aquarium.

Testing and modifying water quality

Modern methods of testing and treating available water for aquarium use make it relatively easy for the fishkeeper to check and improve where necessary. Here we look in detail at hardness, pH (acidity or alkalinity), and then at various contaminants such as iron, copper, chlorine, chloramine, nitrates, nitrites and ammonia. This leads naturally onto the role of aeration and filtration in maintaining a healthy environment for aquarium fishes.

Water hardness

This is the most easily observed quality of water; hard water produces very little lather with soap, soft water seems to produce too much!

Two types of hardness are important to the fishkeeper, namely total or general hardness (sometimes designated as GH) and carbonate hardness (KH), which is also known as alkaline hardness or acid binding capacity (ABC) and, because it is easily removed by boiling, as temporary hardness.

Total hardness is a complex characteristic caused by the presence of various ions of calcium, magnesium, barium and strontium (in that order of importance) associated with sulphates, carbonates, bicarbonates, nitrates and chlorides.

When water is boiled, the bicarbonates of calcium and magnesium, which are quite soluble in water, are decomposed so that virtually all of the barely soluble carbonates are precipitated. This is the cause of the familiar white scale that forms in kettles and hot water

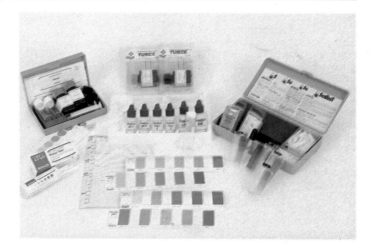

cisterns. The presence of these bicarbonates acts as a reservoir for carbon dioxide in the aquarium and helps to stabilize pH (see page 21).

That fraction of the total hardness that cannot be removed by boiling is called permanent hardness, and is caused principally by calcium sulphate. Permanent hardness can therefore be determined by taking the

Above: *This selection of water test kits includes relatively simple tests to determine pH value, hardness, ammonia, nitrite and nitrate levels.*

figure for temporary hardness from the figure for total hardness.

As well as occurring naturally, hardness can be increased by using inappropriate substrates in aquariums. Marble or dolomite chips, crushed shells or coral sand, for example, will raise the hardness of the water in a freshwater tank by the reaction of small amounts of carbonic

Below: *A jungle stream in Sri Lanka. The high humus levels from decaying plants keep the water soft and acidic – an ideal habitat for Barbs.*

acid in the water with the calcium and magnesium carbonates of the substrates to produce calcium and magnesium bicarbonates. To test gravel, simply add a small quantity of ordinary vinegar (which contains acetic acid) to a sample. If it fizzes then it contains calcium and/or magnesium carbonates and you should think very carefully about the hardening effect it will have on your aquarium water.

Water hardness is expressed in a confusing range of units. In this book we shall use a scale based on milligrams per litre of calcium carbonate (mg/l $CaCO_3$). This is equivalent to parts per million of calcium carbonate (ppm $CaCO_3$).

Some fishes, such as Carp, and most coldwater plants thrive in the hard water conditions found in their natural habitats. However, many organisms are sensitive to excessive hardness, particularly in their early life. Thus, many tropical fishes and plants benefit from living in soft water.

Testing for hardness
It is always a good idea to determine both total and temporary hardness. Various techniques are available for testing water hardness:
1. Using an electronic test meter. This

Above: *Ordinary vinegar added to a sample of gravel will fizz if the gravel contains water-hardening agents, such as calcium carbonate.*

is an elegant, if relatively expensive, way of determining water hardness. The test meter measures the electrical conductivity of the water sample, which is generally in direct proportion to the hardness (i.e. the higher the conductivity the harder the water). This method is usually outside the realm of the amateur aquarist and the results are only relevant when considered with other information. Also, such a simple measurement does not separate total and temporary hardness.
2. Precise tests using indicator solutions, normally carried out in a

COMPARISON OF HARDNESS SCALES

Scale	Origin	Equivalent to	To convert to mg/litre $CaCO_3$ multiply by
°hardness	USA	1mg/litre $CaCO_3$	—
°Clark	UK	14.3mg/litre $CaCO_3$	14.3
°DH	Germany	17.9mg/litre $CaCO_3$	17.9

WATER HARDNESS IN COMMON TERMS

Mg/litre $CaCO_3$	°DH	Considered as
0-50	3	Soft
50-100	3-6	Moderately soft
100-200	6-12	Slightly hard
200-300	12-18	Moderately hard
300-450	18-25	Hard
Over 450	Over 25	Very hard

laboratory. One particular test consists of first adding an indicator to a sample of water; any hardness in the water turns the indicator red. The degree of hardness present is interpreted in terms of the volume of another reagent – the so-called titrant – needed to turn the sample to green.

3. Home test kits. These are less precise versions of the laboratory method described above, but sufficiently accurate for most fishkeeping purposes. Kits are available that measure permanent and temporary hardness separately.

Modifying water hardness

Modifying the hardness of water generally means making it softer. The following methods are available to fishkeepers:

1. Boiling. This will remove temporary hardness only and is not really practical if you have a large aquarium to fill. The chemical reaction that occurs is a reversal of the process by which the temporary hardness is produced.

$Ca(HCO_3)_2 \rightarrow$	$CaCO_3 +$	$H_2O +$	CO_2
Calcium bicarbonate	Calcium carbonate	Water	Carbon dioxide

2. Dilution with soft water. Adding a suitable kind of soft water, such as rainwater, is a cheap and convenient way of reducing water hardness. The hardness is reduced proportionally to the volumes of water mixed together, e.g. Mix 20 litres of rainwater containing 90mg/litre $CaCO_3$ with 10 litres of tapwater containing 300mg/litre $CaCO_3$. The hardness of the 30 litres is now:

$$\frac{20 \times 90 + 10 \times 300}{30} = 160 \text{mg/litre}$$

3. Using a peat filter. Peat has the ability to absorb calcium and also to 'wrap up' calcium ions (technically, to sequester them) so that they are no longer active.

4. Growing duckweed and other plants. Members of the duckweed family, such as *Lemna trisulca*, absorb calcium during their rapid growth and can therefore soften water. *Egeria densa* has the same water-softening effect.

5. Using an ion-exchange resin. In solution salts split up into negatively and positively charged ions. Thus calcium sulphate exists as positive calcium ions (Ca^{++}), so-called cations, and negative sulphate ions (SO_4^{--}), so-called anions. Ion-exchange resins are able to 'capture' these ions from solution and replace them with others, depending on the type of resin. When the resin

Below: *Measuring the electrical conductivity of the aquarium water using an electronic meter is an effective, if relatively expensive, way of determining its hardness.*

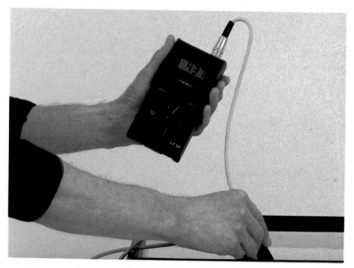

becomes 'full' of captured ions and depleted of the ions it replaces, it can be regenerated by treatment with a suitable chemical solution.

The principle of ion-exchange resins is clear; in reality the choice for fishkeepers is complicated by the chemical results of ion-exchange. For example, ordinary water softening resins are unsuitable for aquarium use because they substitute calcium ions with sodium ions, as shown below:

$CaCO_3 +$	$Na_2R \rightarrow$	$Na_2CO_3 +$	CaR
Calcium carbonate (Permanent hardness)	Sodium resin	Sodium carbonate	Calcium resin

Since sodium carbonate is highly alkaline, the resulting water is totally unsatisfactory for aquarium use.

The most suitable resin is one that replaces calcium ions with hydrogen ions:

$CaCO_3 +$	$H_2R \rightarrow$	$H_2CO_3 +$	CaR
Calcium carbonate	Hydrogen resin	Carbonic acid	Calcium resin

The carbonic acid is unstable and breaks down naturally to produce water and carbon dioxide.

$H_2CO_3 \rightarrow$	$H_2O +$	CO_2
Carbonic acid	Water	Carbon dioxide

The carbon dioxide is used by the plants during photosynthesis or passes into the atmosphere. The resultant water is slightly acid and fairly soft, with a sufficient level of minerals and trace elements to support life.

The so-called 'deionising resins' replace the cations with hydrogen ions (H^+) and the anions with hydroxyl ions (OH^-). These combine to produce chemically pure water that is too depleted of necessary elements for aquarium use. It can be used, however, to dilute other sources of water to soften them.

When using a deionising resin, take care to discard the first few litres since they may contain amines from the resin, which are toxic to fishes. If left

warm and moist, resins can also provide an ideal breeding ground for unwelcome bacteria.

6. Using a reverse-osmosis system. Such a system literally reverses the natural process of osmosis. Pure water separated from a salt solution (i.e. hard water) by a semi-permeable membrane will flow into the solution by the process of osmosis. If a pressure is applied to the salt solution in excess of the osmotic pressure of pure water coming through the membrane, then the flow of pure water is reversed. Although this is an effective method with low running costs, it is extremely expensive to set up in the first place and is probably unnecessarily sophisticated for most fishkeepers to contemplate.

The pH of water

The degree of acidity or alkalinity of water is expressed in terms of pH value, which literally means 'hydrogen power'. It is a logarithmic scale based inversely on the concentration of hydrogen ions in the

water; the more hydrogen ions, the more acid the water and the lower the pH value. The pH scale ranges from 0 (extremely acidic) to 14 (extremely alkaline) with a pH value of 7 as the neutral point.

pH scale

```
0 1 2 3 4 5 6 7 8 9 10 11 12 13 14
              Neutral
Extremely                 Extremely
acidic                    alkaline
```

Since the scale is logarithmic, a pH value of 8 represents a ten-fold decrease in the hydrogen ion concentration compared to a pH value of 7. And a reading of pH9 represents a ten thousand-fold decrease in hydrogen ion concentration compared to a pH value of 5. Therefore, an apparently small sudden change in pH, from say a pH value of 6.5 to a pH value of 8, can cause severe stress to many aquarium fishes.

Above: *Maintaining the correct pH value in a marine aquarium is critical to the well-being of the fishes and the invertebrates it contains. Any adjustment must be made gradually to avoid causing stress.*

It is not surprising, therefore, that inexperienced fishkeepers often kill newly imported fishes through excessive pH change. And conversely, many experienced fishkeepers manage to keep difficult fish successfully by checking the pH of the water regularly.

Many different compounds in water affect its pH. Individual compounds impose a natural but easily disturbed pH value based on their chemical structure; in combination with other substances they establish a more stable pH value less easily disturbed by the addition of other chemicals. Water containing a mix of compounds is said to be 'buffered' to a given pH. The word 'buffer' literally refers to the water's ability to resist change in its pH, just

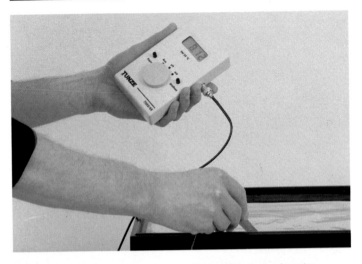

as a buffer on a railway carriage lessens the impact of a collision. Since sea water contains a wide spectrum of dissolved substances it is far more securely 'buffered' against changes in pH than is fresh water. Marine fishes are thus accustomed to a very stable pH value.

Hardness associated with the presence of calcium carbonate produces a hard water with a high pH, i.e. alkaline in nature. Where hardness is caused primarily by calcium sulphate the pH value of the water is generally below 7, depending on other substances present.

Measuring pH
It is possible to measure pH in a number of different ways, depending on how frequently you wish to take readings and how accurate you need the results to be.
1. Using an electronic pH meter. Dipping the electrode into the water provides an instant pH reading. To its credit, this sophisticated device allows you to make repeat measurements as often as you like; its readings are based on the electrical properties of the water. On the debit side, it is relatively expensive for most fishkeepers to buy and needs careful maintenance – particularly of the electrodes – if it is to remain accurate.
2. Using paper strip indicators. The most familiar paper indicator is litmus paper, an obligatory part of our

Above: *This electronic meter registers the pH value of the water directly by measuring electrical activity at the probe. The pH value of 8.1 (i.e. alkaline) is for freshly drawn tapwater. In a mature freshwater aquarium the pH will move towards neutral or slightly acidic.*

childhood excursions into simple science. Paper indicators are available that register more than just 'acid' or 'alkaline', and they are undoubtedly simple and convenient to use. Test for test, however, they work out the most expensive way of taking pH readings.
3. Using a liquid pH test kit. This is the most economical way of measuring pH to a reasonable degree of accuracy. The test consists of adding a few drops of an indicator to a measured sample of water and comparing the colour change to a chart or disc containing coloured 'windows' that represent different pH values. Kits are available that register a broad range of pH values – from pH0 to pH14 – and also narrower ranges for fresh water – from pH4 to pH9 – and for sea water – from pH7.5 to pH9. The only slight difficulty that arises is when the water sample is discoloured, making colour matching rather difficult.

If using any of the above tests shows the water to have a pH value outside the acceptable limits for the

fishes you wish to keep, then you will need to consider modifying the pH in some way.

Modifying pH
Water too acid (i.e. pH too low)
Acid conditions can result from an excess of waste products in the water and are thus more likely to occur in a well-established tank. It is possible, for example, for a natural acid buffer to develop that will resist changes to a more acceptable pH value. An excess of waste products can weaken fishes in the long term, eventually causing disease and death. If you suspect that these conditions apply in your tank, first check the gravel to see if it is abnormally dirty. If you are using an undergravel (biological) filter, check that it is not choked with waste material from the fishes

Since a complete and sudden water change would cause pH shock, consider the following less drastic measures to restore the pH balance.
1. Using an automatic water changer. This is an ideal way of introducing mains water slowly into the tank until a preset amount of old water has been replaced. It works entirely automatically and is operated by water pressure alone.
2. Replacing approximately 25 percent of the tank water every day for a week with water of suitable quality. This may mean using

Above: *Taking a pH reading using paper strip indicators involves dipping the strip into the water for a few moments and then comparing its colour change to a printed chart. Such indicators are widely available to cover specific ranges in pH value for both fresh and salt water.*

rainwater, for example, for which an automatic water changer cannot easily be used.
3. Using a filter containing zeolite and carbon in conjunction with some water changing. This combined filter removes most harmful waste products and thus reduces acidity, as explained in more detail on page 28 and 33. Zeolite does not work in sea water, however.
4. Filtering the water through marble chips or dolomite as well as through zeolite. This will remove waste products and increase the hardness (and raise the pH) at the same time.
5. Adding sodium carbonate or trisodium phosphate to increase alkalinity but not hardness.
Water too alkaline (i.e. pH too high)
To reduce the alkalinity try the following:
1. Replacing some of the water with softer water (usually more acidic in nature). You can use rainwater or soft water prepared by boiling or after treatment with an ion-exchange resin (see page 20).

2. Adding monosodium dihydrogen phosphate or dilute phosphoric acid. These will reduce alkalinity without affecting the hardness of the water. Always use such additives with caution, particularly phosphoric acid, which you should use in dilute form only and add drop by drop to avoid rapid pH changes.
3. Use a peat filter (page 34).

Iron compounds
The reddish colour of the bed of tropical streams is caused by precipitation of iron compounds. Many tropical plants need a relatively high iron concentration (1mg/litre expressed as the metal) in order to achieve lush growth. However, this iron has to be present as a combination with organic substances, not simply an iron solution added to the water.

Iron may be present in aquarium water from several sources: it may occur naturally; it may have contaminated water that has run through iron pipes; or it may be derived from rusty angle-iron frames, although these are now rarely seen.

Tests are available to determine iron concentration, but these are not really necessary for the average aquarist since it is unlikely that the levels of iron will be sufficiently high to cause distress to the fishes.

Copper compounds
Some copper compounds are used as treatments for certain fish diseases. These should be used with care, however, since many freshwater fishes are distressed by a copper level of 0.5mg/l and marine fishes are sensitive to copper at concentrations as low as 0.1mg/l. Proprietary treatments for disease organisms such as *Oodinium* sp., which causes velvet disease and coral fish disease, overcome this problem by using more sophisticated and safer copper compounds.

As we have seen, using tapwater that has been standing in copper pipes – particularly in soft water areas – may lead to unacceptable levels of copper in the aquarium. It is wise to run some to waste before using it for the aquarium.

Above: *The level of chlorine in tap-water can be reduced by standing and aeration or by adding a few drops of a commercial anti-chlorine product to the aquarium, as shown here.*

Chlorine and chloramine

Chlorine added to tapwater as a disinfectant is easily dispersed either by standing, and preferably aerating, the water for 24 hours, or by adding an anti-chlorine compound. Commercial anti-chlorine products are generally based on sodium thiosulphate, but modern formulations contain other compounds, such as protective colloids, designed to reduce the stress on the fishes caused by 'raw' tapwater.

Chlorine added to water reacts with any ammonia present to form chloramines. These compounds are ideal as disinfectants, since they take longer to disperse. In fact, some water authorities add ammonia to the chlorinated water to actively encourage the formation of chloramine. Unfortunately, this is hardly ideal for fishkeepers.

Below: *The elegant corals that grace marine aquariums are particularly sensitive to high levels of nitrate in the water. Take frequent readings and gradual appropriate action.*

Chloramine can be removed either by aerating the water for a much longer period than is usually required to disperse chlorine (between two and five days, depending on circumstances) or by using a chlorine remover together with a zeolite or zeolite/carbon filter.

Ammonia, nitrites and nitrates

Among the most important aspects of water quality for the fishkeeper to consider are the levels of ammonia, nitrites and nitrates. All these compounds are produced at different stages of the nitrogen cycle – a natural sequence of events in which nitrogen is incorporated into a wide range of simple inorganic substances and complex organic molecules vital to all living processes. Once formed, nitrogen compounds are fairly reactive but pure nitrogen gas, which makes up four-fifths of the atmosphere, is relatively inert and resists combination with other elements.

Nitrogen enters the nitrogen cycle in two main ways: mainly through the actions of nitrogen-fixing bacteria –

THE NITROGEN CYCLE

This simplified version of the nitrogen cycle shows how nitrogen circulates in the natural world. The important stages for fishkeepers are those involving the conversion of toxic ammonium compounds by bacterial action to nitrites and nitrates.

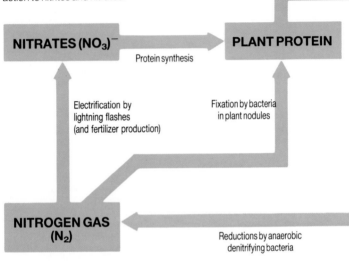

NITRATES (NO_3)⁻ → PLANT PROTEIN

Protein synthesis

Electrification by lightning flashes (and fertilizer production)

Fixation by bacteria in plant nodules

NITROGEN GAS (N_2)

Reductions by anaerobic denitrifying bacteria

notably those in the nodules of leguminous plants – and to a lesser degree by fusion with oxygen in the high-energy conditions of lightning flashes (so-called 'electrification'). The simple oxides of nitrogen formed in the atmosphere by electrification dissolve in water vapour to form acids. These fall to earth and readily react with minerals to form nitrates, especially calcium nitrate.

The nitrates form plant food – hence the nitrate fertilizers widely used by farmers – and the nitrogen is built up into amino acids and plant proteins. Animals eating the plant proteins convert them into animal proteins. Through animal waste products and from the decay of dead plants and animals, the nitrogen passes into simpler and simpler compounds. Paramount among

these are ammonium compounds formed from ammonia (NH_3), a highly reactive gas that readily dissolves in water and is extremely toxic to animal life. Ammonium compounds and similar substances are oxidised by bacteria into nitrites (NO_2) and then into nitrates (NO_3). Nitrates are used as plant food and enter the nitrogen cycle once again. A proportion, however, are broken down by bacteria living in the absence of oxygen into free nitrogen gas.

In the natural world this process goes on continuously in all terrestrial and aquatic environments. In the closed confines of the aquarium, however, the fishkeeper must play a vital part in maintaining a healthy balance of nitrogenous compounds. Nitrogen-containing food added to the aquarium eventually becomes

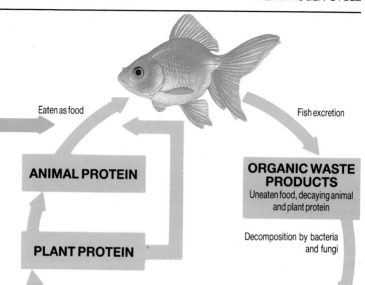

Eaten as food

Fish excretion

ANIMAL PROTEIN

ORGANIC WASTE PRODUCTS
Uneaten food, decaying animal and plant protein

PLANT PROTEIN

Decomposition by bacteria and fungi

Protein synthesis

AMMONIA (NH_3) AND SIMILAR COMPOUNDS

NITRATES (NO_3)⁻

Oxidation by nitrifying bacteria, such as *Nitrobacter* sp.

NITRITES (NO_2)⁻

Oxidation by nitrifying bacteria, such as *Nitrosomonas* sp.

organic waste, either as waste products from the fishes or as uneaten remains of food or in the form of decaying plants and animals.

Much of this organic matter can be removed by mechanical filtration (see page 31). What remains decomposes by bacterial action into ammonia or ammonia-like compounds, which are highly toxic to aquatic life. It is therefore important that the growth of nitrifying bacteria (such as *Nitrosomonas* sp.) is encouraged, since these combine the ammonia with oxygen in the water to form nitrites, which are slightly less toxic. Nitrites are then converted by further bacteria (such as *Nitrobacter* sp.) with the addition of more oxygen into nitrates, which are much less toxic.

Resistance to these compounds varies according to species. Some

corals, and fishes such as Discus in freshwater and Moorish Idols in saltwater, for example, do not tolerate more than about 20mg/l of nitrate. Goldfishes will tolerate 500mg/l, although a high nitrate level will cause stress and inevitably raise their susceptibility to disease.

In freshwater aquariums, the addition of a small quantity of salt, say 0.3 percent (3 grams per litre; 2¾ teaspoons per gallon) will reduce the effect of nitrite on most fishes. Kits are available for measuring the levels of ammonia, nitrite and nitrate in aquarium water. These are essential for use in marine aquariums, and valuable for the serious freshwater aquarist.

It is reasonably easy to keep down the levels of ammonia and nitrite in the aquarium by using undergravel filters

Above: *This nitrite test begins with adding seven drops of the first reagent to a 5ml sample of water.*

Above: *After 10 seconds it is time to add seven drops of the second reagent and shake the sample well.*

Above: *Two minutes later comparison with a colour chart shows the level of nitrite. Similar tests determine pH value and hardness.*

or one of the modern biological filtration methods. There are also claims that some biological systems also remove nitrates, but the technology is not yet fully advanced. Also, denitrifying bacteria (those that convert nitrate to nitrogen gas) grow naturally in the gravel, living in the absence of oxygen.

In freshwater aquariums, nitrates can be removed along with any stray ammonium compounds and nitrites by using zeolite in the filter. Activated carbon is sometimes mixed with this to remove some other impurities at the same time. The traditional method of removing nitrate is to carry out partial water changes – approximately 20-25 percent of the aquarium water every 3-4 weeks. Be careful not to do this too rapidly, however, since this may cause undue stress to the fishes.

Osmosis

Osmosis is a concept we have discussed briefly in connection with water hardness. Here we consider the implications of osmosis principally from the fishes' point of view.

Any substance dissolved in water will have a natural tendency to dilute itself by pulling in any surrounding water molecules. When solutions of different strengths are separated by a semi-permeable membrane (a cell membrane, for example) pure water flows from the weaker solution to dilute the stronger one until they are both the same strength. This natural movement of water is called osmosis and the pressure it creates is known as osmotic pressure.

Osmosis is very important to fishes. The body fluid of freshwater fishes is generally more concentrated than the surrounding water. Therefore, water moves by osmosis through the semi-permeable membranes of the gills and skin and constantly dilutes their body fluids. Freshwater fishes, therefore, excrete waste water in the form of a dilute urine to prevent themselves becoming 'waterlogged'.

Marine fishes, in general, must cope with the reverse situation; sea water has a higher concentration of dissolved salts than the body fluids and marine fishes must therefore

FRESHWATER FISH

MARINE FISH

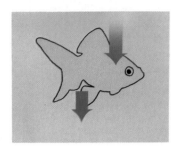

Above: *A freshwater fish (left) constantly absorbs water into its body by the natural processs of osmosis. A marine fish (right) loses water by the same process and must drink heavily to compensate.*

Below: *A healthy Discus in ideal aquarium conditions. This delicate freshwater tropical species will thrive in a deep tank with soft, slightly acidic, very clean water – ideally filtered through peat.*

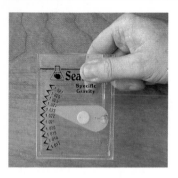 

Above: *Two ways of testing specific gravity in a marine aquarium: with a swing-needle device (left) or using a floating hydrometer (right).*

drink copiously to avoid 'drying out'. Since they are drinking sea water, they must separate out the pure water and excrete relatively small quantities of concentrated urine.

The concentration of a solution can be broadly interpreted in terms of its specific gravity. Too rapid a change in specific gravity, and therefore in osmotic pressure, can cause severe, often fatal, 'osmotic shock' to most fishes. In marine aquariums, specific gravity of the water can be easily checked with a hydrometer, either the conventional floating type or a swing-needle device. Transferring fishes from one aquarium to another of equal specific gravity should cause no osmotic shock at all.

In freshwater aquariums, the addition of common salt (sodium chloride) to the water reduces the osmotic pressure between the aquarium water and the body fluids of the fish. While some fishes are happier in slightly salty water in any case, the addition of a small quantity of salt when the fishes are off-colour, injured or have ulcers reduces the osmotic stress upon them. In other words, they do not have to use up so much energy excreting large quantities of water entering the body due to osmosis. The recommended strength as a general aquarium additive is 0.1 percent solution (i.e. 1 gm/litre or approximately 1 teaspoon per gallon).

Even more effective than common salt alone is a mixture of common salt

with about 1.2 percent potassium chloride and 1.7 percent calcium chloride, making a 'physiological' solution for aquarium use.

Aeration and filtration
This section focuses on the practical relationship between aeration and filtration in water chemistry.

As we have seen, in the confines of an aquarium the natural biological processes that purify the water cannot take place without a little outside help from the fishkeeper. In nature, there is space for decomposition products to be oxidised and converted naturally to nitrates. The nitrates, in turn, may be either washed away by running water or by rains or converted into luxuriant plant growth. Aquarium technology has now developed to a point where such purification processes can easily be simulated in the aquarium.

The objects of aeration and filtration may be considered as:
1. To increase the oxygen content of the water, both for the direct benefit of the fishes and to aid the nitrification of waste products.
2. To remove waste material mechanically, chemically and biologically.

Aeration
Aeration may be carried out during the actual filtration process, or it may be provided separately. The aim is to allow oxygen to diffuse into the water and waste gases, such as carbon dioxide and ammonia, to diffuse out. An air pump may be used to provide air bubbles through a diffuser, usually an airstone. In marine aquariums, where adequate aeration and

filtration are especially critical, powerheads containing a motor driven impeller may be used to circulate the water and draw in air at the same time.

The extent to which gases diffuse in and out of the water depends upon the area of water in contact with the air. The normal stream of bubbles usually seen in freshwater aquariums provides only a small direct interface between the air and the water. It is the circulation of the water in the aquarium caused by the rising bubbles that brings about the most significant interchange at the water surface.

Aerators without filters therefore provide useful gaseous interchange but, even with regular water changes, they are rarely sufficient to maintain adequate biological conditions within the aquarium. Some method of water filtration is also necessary.

Below: *The rising flow of bubbles in an airlift tube creates a beneficial circulation in an aquarium, keeping the water aerated at the surface.*

Mechanical and chemical filtration

This is based on the concept of removing water from the main body of the aquarium, processing it to remove waste products, and returning it to the aquarium, preferably aerating it at the same time. Such filters basically consist of an open or closed box containing filter media, through which the water is drawn either by the water-flow set up by a stream of bubbles from an air pump or by using a small electrically driven centrifugal pump.

The simplest filter of this type is the air-operated box filter for use inside the aquarium. It removes the dirt mechanically, at the same time providing water circulation and aeration. External open-box filters clipped on the side of the tank provide similar facilities. These can be air-powered or fitted with an electrically driven impeller. Other motor filters – so-called power filters – consist of a closed box, either with some device for incorporating air into the water stream or with a spray bar to break up the surface as water returns to the aquarium. This forms an effective way of aerating the water.

For most purposes, the aquarist has a choice of suitable filter media. To remove dirt mechanically, various grades of filter wool (usually man-made fibres, such as dacron floss, nylon floss, etc.) are available. These should be specified very carefully by the manufacturer, since harmful compounds are frequently used as antistatic agents. As a precaution, always wash any filter wool thoroughly before use. The grade of wool chosen is really a matter of personal experiment. Ideally, the wool should be fine enough to trap even quite small dirt particles and yet allow free flow of water through the filter. Also for economy, the wool should be capable of being washed clean several times before being discarded. Sometimes, filter pads cut to size may be provided.

Filter foam is useful, not only as a mechanical filter, but also as a medium which will sustain a substantial colony of nitrifying bacteria, so providing a useful

biological filter. Some filters even consist basically of a body composed of foam. The quality of the foam is very important since many polyurethane foams (as used in furniture) are toxic to fishes.

Filter carbon is commonly placed in the filter body under the wool or foam. There are many grades of carbon or

Left: *A simple external box filter packed with activated carbon, zeolite granules (in perforated plastic sachets) and a layer of filter wool.*

Below: *To maintain the precise conditions necessary in a marine aquarium, more complex filtration systems are usually needed. Here an external biological and an algal filter operate below the tank.*

charcoal, not all of which are entirely suitable for aquarium filtration. Some make the water highly alkaline and are specifically designed for marine use. The degree of alkaline reaction can be shown by measuring the pH value of a small sample of water before and after adding some of the carbon. Other grades of carbon are not properly activated; at one time even ordinary wood charcoal was sold for aquarium use. As a relative test of activity make up a weak solution of methylene blue and add this drop by drop to a sample of water containing the carbon and note the point at which the blue colour is not totally cleared by the carbon. The activation process – basically baking the carbon at high temperature – opens up minute pores in the granules, so presenting a very large surface to the water. This high-temperature treatment also activates the surface area so that it readily adsorbs certain materials. (Note: adsorb indicates that the substance is taken up by the surface area of the medium, rather than simply absorbed like a sponge.)

Activated carbon therefore has two main functions. Firstly, it will adsorb waste materials, thus helping to purify the water. This can be a disadvantage, however, when treating the aquarium with disease remedies because the carbon adsorbs the medicaments before they have their intended effect on the fishes. Also, certain medications, such as those containing phenoxyethanol, will displace previously adsorbed waste products

Below: *For fry-raising tanks only a simple sponge filter is necessary to keep the water clean. This system will not trap fry and provides beneficial surface water flow across the tank.*

Below: *This electrically driven internal filter draws tank water in at the bottom, through the filter medium and out at the top. Air is added to the out-going stream of water.*

Above: *Some basic filter materials. The filter wool (usually a synthetic floss) traps dirt particles. Zeolite granules (packed in sachets) and activated carbon both help to extract dissolved waste products from water.*

Below: *A relative test of activated carbons using methylene blue. Complete adsorption (left) leaves the water clear. A less efficient carbon (right) fails to remove all the pigment and inconveniently floats.*

from the carbon, so releasing a large quantity of potentially toxic substances into the aquarium at one time. It is therefore essential to remove activated carbon from a filter system before using any medication.

The second use for activated carbon is as a biological medium. Because of the vast area in contact with the water, a small amount of carbon can act as a vast biological bed for nitrifying bacteria. There is

also a suspicion that denitrification could take place in certain circumstances, i.e. the conversion of nitrates into nitrogen gas by bacteria in the absence of oxygen.

Fibrous peat from high moorland areas is sometimes used as a filtration medium. It is one of nature's own ion-exchange materials and is capable of softening the water. It contains humic acid and other organic acids which lower the pH, particularly of soft water. It also contains substances related to vitamins and hormones, and many fishes and plants thrive in peat-treated water. The disinfectant action can be illustrated by considering the number of perfectly preserved corpses recovered from peat bogs.

Among more specialized filtration media available are ion-exchange resins. As we have seen earlier, some of these need to be treated with caution, since they can remove too much of the desirable minerals and trace elements in aquarium water.

Another style of mechanical filter, designed for use in marine aquariums, is the protein skimmer. This device consists of a vertical reactor tube with a constant stream of air bubbles rising within it. Organic waste material separates out in the froth that forms at the top of the tube and collects in a separate container around the rim.

An ozonizer is often used in conjunction with a protein skimmer.

Ozone (O_3) – an unstable form of oxygen that acts as a powerful disinfectant – is generated in the ozonizer from air passed through an electrical discharge. It quickly reverts to normal oxygen, however, and so it is fed directly to the central column of the protein skimmer, but never into the aquarium. Since ozone is harmful to all living organisms, it must be used with the utmost caution.

Water can also be effectively sterilized by intense ultraviolet light, a process employed in the UV sterilizers used in marine aquariums and in freshwater commercial installations where recirculation water is required.

Biological filters

The principle of biological filters is to build up in the filter medium a colony of friendly bacteria to break down waste products – specifically to carry out the nitrification process and, hopefully in some cases, also denitrification.

Below: *Filtration systems for marine aquariums can be very sophisticated. This one includes a digital readout of* *temperature, a pH meter, and a dosing pump to dispense liquid treatments into the aquarium.*

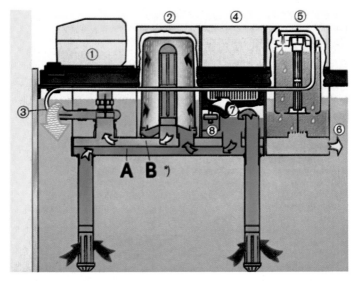

Above: *This advanced filtration system combines mechanical and biological filtration functions in one unit, plus automatic water level regulation. Tank water drawn in by the centrifugal pump (1) passes through channel A to a mechanical filter (2). Part of the water flow is directed via channel B out across the water surface (3) to promote aeration; the remainder is pumped to a biological filter unit (5). Here the water flow is reduced to a steady trickle onto porous clay granules. In the upper portion of this unit, where air can reach the granules, a colony of oxygen-breathing bacteria converts ammonium wastes to nitrates. In the submerged portion of the unit bacteria living in the absence of oxygen convert some of these nitrates to free nitrogen gas. The purified water leaves at the base (6). The water level regulator (4) and the associated water flow (7) and sensor device (8) are shown at above right.*

Above: *A close view of the hardware described at top. From the left: main pump, quick-change filter, water level regulator, biological filter, pump for the protein skimmer (mainly marines).*

Right: *The complex filtration system (plus protein skimmer) featured on these pages is ideal for maintaining the fine environmental balance essential in this marine aquarium.*

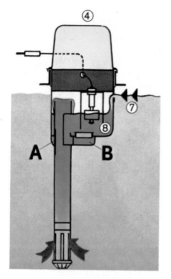

Left: *This side view highlights the water level regulator (4) of the system shown opposite. The water level in the tank is maintained such that water just laps over into the unit. A floating sensor (8) registers the level in a special chamber and sends back electrical signals to a dosing pump if there is any drop. The dosing pump replenishes water lost by evaporation and can also be used to administer fertilizers and other chemicals. It is important to maintain the water level (especially in marine tanks) because it alters the osmotic concentration in the aquarium.*

Below: *The complete system, including (at far right) a protein skimmer with associated pump. The protein skimmer removes organic matter on a rising mass of bubbles.*

Although some foam filters and carbon filter media also show a biological action, by far the most widely used biological filter in freshwater and marine aquariums is the undergravel filter. Most undergravel filters depend upon water being drawn from underneath a filter plate, either with an airlift consisting of a vertical tube into which air bubbles are released, or by means of a powerhead – a small electrically driven impeller mounted on top of the vertical tube. The aquarium water is thus drawn down into the gravel bed, which not only filters the water mechanically but also allows the bacteria that have built up in the gravel to break down and nitrify the organic waste material.

The effectiveness of an undergravel filter depends on the nature of the gravel substrate; the more porous the substrate the more effective the nitrifying process. In marine aquariums, coral sand is particularly favoured because this also acts as a buffering agent in helping to stabilize the pH of the water (see page 21).

The main advantage of undergravel filters is that they are virtually maintenance-free for reasonably long periods. After one or two years, however, the system usually needs breaking down completely for cleaning. And plant growth may suffer because of the constant flow of water past the roots.

A mechanical filter may be used in conjunction with an undergravel filter to pre-clean the water before it is circulated in the opposite direction, i.e. upwards through the gravel from underneath the plate. This is known as a reverse-flow undergravel filtration system and has the advantage of excellent biological action without the disadvantage of dirt becoming trapped in the gravel. The whole system can therefore function for a much longer time before needing an overhaul.

Right: *Cleaning the gravel with this device is simply a matter of drawing batches of gravel up into the siphonic water flow so that suspended dirt is rapidly whisked away.*

Below: *This compact filtration unit is built in as part of the tank and can be tailored in complexity to suit various fishes' requirements – including marines. The composite cutaway features the following points: 1 Protein skimmer (mainly for marines) 2 Quick-change pre-filter 3 Water inlet from tank 4 Undergravel filter plate 5 Substrate 6 Heater-thermostat 7 Air diffuser 8 Water outlet under filter plate 9 Water pumps 10 Contra-flow aeration 11 Water outlet into tank.*

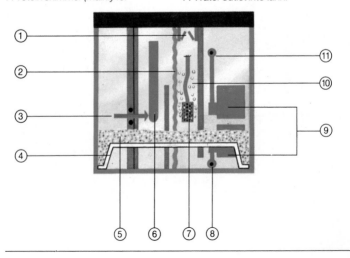

There are sometimes unaccountable outbreaks of disease in aquariums with undergravel filters. The problem is almost certainly caused by the lack of regular cleaning and the build up of undesirable products within the aquarium.

Hopefully, this brief look at the basic chemical properties of water and their implications will provide a useful background to help you maintain a healthy aquarium.

Below: *This diagram shows how the water circulates in a reverse-flow filtration system using the hardware featured at bottom left. Water taken into the unit (1) is heated, mechanically filtered, aerated and passed through a protein skimmer (if applicable) and pumped back into the aquarium upwards through the undergravel filter plate (2). This pre-cleaning helps to reduce routine maintenance of the undergravel filter. Water is also pumped into the tank at a higher level (3) to help circulation.*

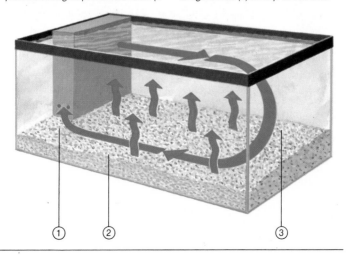

Growing Healthy Aquarium Plants

Many attractive varieties of plants are available for the home freshwater aquarium to challenge the skills of even the most ambitious and expert of potential growers. In some countries, particularly in Holland and Germany, for example, raising an aquarium brimful with exquisite plants has become an end in itself; local and national competitions are fiercely contested. These truly supreme displays of lush vegetation invariably act as a magnificent foil for a few really healthy fishes, thus epitomising the natural balance that exists between fishes and plants in their wild habitats. With a little care and some help from modern aquarium equipment every fishkeeper can emulate these results.

It is quite extraordinary how well some plants adapt to living in the aquarium environment, often acquiring quite distinct characteristics, so that it is hard to recognise them as the same species compared to their wild forms. And plants need not be solely con-

fined to below the water level; many aquarium plants are marsh plants that will eagerly provide an interesting display out of the water, often bursting into flower.

Of course, conditions in the aquarium must suit the plants selected to soften its harsh edges. Sometimes, however, it is difficult to see why plants in seemingly identical tanks offering comparable conditions fare so differently. In one tank, the plants may flourish; in the other, they may simply waste away from the moment they are planted. In this brief section, we explore the reasons for success or failure with aquarium plants, touching on the importance of preparing the tank well beforehand, the best choices of substrate and filtration systems, the hazards posed by introduced pests and diseases, the influence of lighting levels, and new techniques to promote plant growth. These points may help you to provide a sumptuous living background for your aquarium fishes.

Every fishkeeper looks forward to owning an aquarium abundantly stocked with healthy, growing plants. Not only are plants decorative and fascinating in their own right but they also contribute to the overall health of the aquarium in many important ways. Unfortunately, many aquarists find that growing plants successfully is one of the most difficult techniques to master. And with the advent of super-realistic plastic plants, one wonders how much of this luxuriant growth is genuine in every instance!

Above: *Raising and maintaining such a splendid array of real plants in a freshwater tropical aquarium provides a challenge for fishkeepers.*

The case for plastic plants
There is actually a good reason for using at least a proportion of plastic plants in an aquarium. The large

Below: *These plastic plants have been 'planted' literally in moments. The base plate of one cluster can be seen half buried in the gravel.*

surface area of the plastic fronds soon becomes covered with a plaque of beneficial nitrifying bacteria that help to reduce the levels of ammonia and nitrites in the aquarium. The plants thus make an extremely efficient integral biological filter. Plastic plants are not sensitive to water, to the lighting or to the planting medium and they can provide cover for the fishes if provided in sufficient quantity.

However, what plastic plants cannot do on their own is to promote a balanced aquarium by removing excess mineral salts, nitrates and other organic materials used by growing plants as fertilizers. In an aquarium fully stocked only with plastic plants, these functions have to be carried out artificially by using a carbon/zeolite filter medium or by making more frequent water changes than usual.

You can't beat real plants!
Although plastic plants have their benefits, growing plants add a charisma to the aquarium which cannot be achieved in any other way. There are many attractive species available, and most fishkeepers find it a satisfying challenge to grow them successfully in their own tanks.

Below: *After a few weeks in the aquarium these plastic plants have become coated in a layer of bacteria that help to purify the water.*

Real plants help to purify the water by using waste materials, such as nitrates, in their growth. They also provide shelter for timid adults and, floating plants particularly, for fry. The algae and minute organisms that live on and around the plants provide food for many fishes. And many difficult fishes will only spawn on real plants. The extra maintenance needed to keep plants growing properly may seem an irksome chore to lazy fishkeepers, but the rewards seem to outweigh the disadvantages. Possibly, the ideal combination is to use some plastic plants to provide a nitrifying function and a selection of real plants to help remove waste materials from the water.

Preparing for the plants
Preparing the aquarium for good plant growth centres on water quality and the planting medium. Most aquarium plants prefer moderately soft water with a pH of 6.8 to 7.0. Some plants, notably *Egeria densa* and *Ceratophyllum* sp., thrive in hard, alkaline water with a pH value in the region of 8.0. If you really wish to grow plants in a serious way, carry out some basic research to check on their individual requirements.

The basic choices of planting medium are clean sand or gravel. These may be used in conjunction with some clay, loam or peat, depending upon the plants to be grown and the type of filtration system fitted in the tank. Many aquatic plants use their roots primarily for anchorage and absorb at least a proportion of their nutrients directly through the leaves. In the right conditions, some plants will flourish without being rooted at all. Most tropical plants like warm roots, and the gravel in a tropical aquarium may be considerably cooler than the rest of the environment. This problem may be overcome either by using a base heater, which fits under the aquarium, or by using a cable heater buried in the gravel. When using such heaters, always ensure that the gravel is sufficiently deep to avoid burning the roots (see below). The most usual solution, however, is to fit an undergravel (biological) filter.

Above: *'Aquascaping' a tank with plants can be as creative as it is beneficial in providing a well-balanced environment for the fishes.*

An undergravel filter (see page 38) can maintain warm roots by circulating the aquarium water through the planting medium. Some aquarists claim that many plants will

Below: *Floating water hyacinths on a river in Thailand. Many aquarium plants are raised from wild forms collected from such tropical areas.*

not grow successfully with a constant flow of water past their roots, but general experience shows that most plants prosper in aquariums fitted with undergravel filters. If the water flow does cause problems then one possible solution is to place some form of solid barrier over an appropriate part of the filter plate. Be sure to use a thick layer of planting medium over the plate – 7.5-10cm (3-4in) is ideal. Prepared fibrous peat can be placed on the filter plate below the gravel. Do not use clay or loam in aquariums with undergravel filters,

Above: *Be sure to buy plants from dealers who keep them planted in fresh and healthy conditions; they will establish that much quicker.*

although these substrates are generally suitable for other filters.

If you are uncertain about the gravel, try testing a sample with ordinary vinegar as explained on page 18. If the gravel fizzes (due to the action of acetic acid) this indicates a high calcium content, which may be desirable for calcium-loving plants but entirely unsuitable for other types of plants. Your dealer should be able to supply calcium-free gravel.

Various fertilizers are available to give your plants a good start. They are especially important in 'clinical' set-ups with washed, calcium-free substrates, water with a low mineral content and no peat or other organic planting medium. Plants can also be encouraged to grow by placing them in blocks of organic material in the form of plugs or pillows. These are ideal for use in new tanks in which sufficient detritus has yet to build up to provide a natural supply of fertilizers for the plants.

Treating plants

The most common pests introduced with plants into the aquarium are *Hydra*, which can attack young fishes, and leeches, which can be a menace on larger fishes. Snails are also easily introduced with plants and, although undesirable in the breeding tank, are otherwise generally harmless. Plants destined for the garden pond may also harbour a range of undesirable creatures that may cause problems.

The potential hazard from introduced pests depends on the source of live plants. Those collected from the wild (check that you are not breaking the law in doing so) are more likely to carry pests than those obtained from your dealer. In any event, it is wise to inspect all plants carefully and to clean them thoroughly before use.

Before cleaning plants check that they are in good condition. If they have been kept unplanted and crowded in a tank for several days, they are less likely to become established than when kept properly planted. To clean live plants, wash them in 'off-cold' fresh water at about 22°C (72°F), ideally containing a plant cleaning agent. This may be one of the special commercial preparations, but sufficient potassium permanganate crystals to colour the water pale pink is an effective alternative. Be sure to rinse the plants thoroughly in fresh water after treatment with chemicals.

Clean plastic plants by washing them in warm water containing sufficient domestic bleach to disinfect them. Then wash them very well in running water until all traces of the bleach have been removed before introducing them to the tank. Check first on one plant that the bleach does not harm the plastic material.

Lighting for plant growth

Providing good lighting for plant growth is a question of striking a balance between the demands of the plants; the type, intensity and duration of the lighting; and the size and depth of the tank. Some plants thrive in brighter light than others, for example, and deep tanks generally need more intense lighting than shallow ones.

Daylight, without too much direct sunlight, is ideal for plant growth in aquariums. It is difficult to control the intensity and duration of daylight,

however, and direct sunshine may overheat the water and cause excessive growth of algae. The duration of daylight is a particular problem during the winter in higher latitudes (ie, away from the Equator). While plants do need a dark period each day, winter daylight cannot provide the minimum of 10 hours light that most plants must have for good growth. The solution, therefore, is to use an artificial form of lighting.

The most popular and effective form of artificial lighting is provided by fluorescent tubes. There are several types available which are excellent for plant growth, ranging from the Grolux types with a pinkish hue to those that simulate the entire spectrum of natural daylight. Although fluorescent

Below: *Dutch aquariums reign supreme in the world for the quality and care of their planting and decoration, as this example shows.*

lighting is more costly to install than using tungsten incandescent lamps, it does score on being relatively cheap to run and cool in operation.

Judging the exact amount of lighting required is often a matter of trial and error. As an approximate guide, an aquarium 60cm (24in) long and 30cm (12in) deep needs two 40-watt tungsten lamps or one 20-watt fluorescent tube. The formula on which this is calculated recommends 40 watts of tungsten light or 10 watts of fluorescent light for every 30cm (12in) of aquarium length.

More intense lighting, especially suitable for marine aquariums that attempt to simulate the brightness of a coral reef, can be provided by mercury vapour and metal halide lamps. These lamps produce a wide spectrum of wavelengths to encourage good plant growth and are particularly good for illuminating relatively deep tanks.

Whatever type of lighting you choose, always insert a transparent barrier, such as a cover glass, between the light source and the water surface to guard against splashing and condensation on live electrical circuits.

New techniques for plant growth
New ways of encouraging plants to grow in the aquarium are currently being developed. For instance, it has been found that the amount of carbon dioxide (CO_2) produced as a by-product of the fishes' metabolism is not usually sufficient to promote maximum plant growth. To supplement natural supplies, carbon dioxide gas can be fed into the tank using a special diffuser. This must be properly controlled, however, to avoid endangering the fishes. Other developments include the use of fertilizers containing iron compounds in a particularly effective form.

Improving Success with Fishbreeding

Some fishkeepers seem to have the 'magic touch'; they appear able to breed any fish with little apparent effort. But look a little closer and you may see the evidence of more care than seemed obvious at first sight. Here we probe into those little touches that seem to make all the difference between success and failure in fishbreeding. A challenge made more interesting by the capricious variations in behaviour between species and even between individuals of the same species.

The first step to consider is the preparation of the breeding tank. And in this respect the psychological aspects are every bit as important as the purely physical or chemical ones. Unless the prospective parents are at ease in their surroundings, the chances of successful breeding are virtually nil. Next, always select your breeding fishes with care. If you are breeding livebearers, then choose healthy, adult or semi-adult fishes with good colour and

excellent body shape. If the fishes are group spawners, then leave only the best fishes in the breeding tank. Fishes that spawn in pairs tend to select their own mates. Ideally, buy several young fishes, grow them on and allow the best ones to pair up.

To prepare fishes for breeding feed them up beforehand on live foods, or certain kinds of frozen, freeze-dried or processed foods can be equally nutritious. Make sure the conditions for spawning are just right and then consider your provisions for hatching and aftercare of the fry. All these stages, each with its own particular problems and techniques, add up to the stimulating challenge that fishbreeding provides. Following the tips and general advice given in this section should give you a useful start in fishbreeding. And if you want to pursue the subject further, the relevant books listed under Additional Reading on page 112 will provide a great deal of helpful information on all aspects of this fascinating subject.

The willingness of fishes to breed in the aquarium is influenced to a great extent by various environmental factors, such as the way in which the aquarium is furnished, the selection and prior treatment of the fishes before breeding is attempted, the quality and temperature of the water, lighting and feeding. Pests and diseases are also a constant source of danger to the newly developing fishes in an aquartium.

Many books are available that deal with individual types or species of fishes, and these usually give specific breeding requirements for the group concerned. Studying such specialist references will provide valuable, if at times conflicting, information. Only practical experience can help you to find the best method of breeding a certain type of fish.

Breeding is an exciting aspect of fishkeeping; here we consider briefly the influence of a number of environmental factors, water chemistry and disease on successful breeding in the home aquarium.

The influence of aquascaping

A fully furnished aquarium that is ideal for displaying the adult fishes may be hardly conducive to successful breeding. Understandably, many aquariums are furnished so that a large open space is provided at the front of the tank where, ideally, the fishes will show themselves from time to time. Many fishes are highly territorial, however, and such an arrangement of rocks and plants may not provide a sufficient number of suitable individual territories to make the fishes feel at home and therefore likely to breed.

The plants in many show aquariums may be unsuitable even for hiding baby livebearers – which are almost immediately able to fend for themselves – and the other

Below: *A male Siamese Fighting Fish builds a nest of bubbles and plant fragments on the water surface. He will guard the 400-500 eggs that the female lays in the nest and chaperone the fry when they hatch out.*

Above: *A male Orange Chromide guards his fry. Plants in the aquarium provide essential hiding places to make young fishes feel secure.*

inhabitants may be either too aggressive or too greedy to allow many of the babies to survive in the relatively small confines of the aquarium. This problem may be overcome to some extent by using a breeding trap, but the ideal solution is to provide a separate breeding tank. The efficient filtration systems fitted in some display aquariums may also cause problems because they filter out the supply of tiny planktonic organisms on which baby fishes feed.

Floating plants represent another possible source of conflict between the aims of display and breeding tanks. Conditions may not be suitable for them in some tanks or, at the other extreme, they may grow so vigorously that they block off valuable light and need constant culling to keep them in check. And yet many nest-building fishes, such as Gouramies, may only breed successfully with a plentiful supply of floating plants.

Many fishes require something to remind them of their natural habitat in order to induce them to breed. Angelfishes, for instance, will seek broad-leaved plants or even a strip of slate or glass on which to lay their adhesive eggs, which they will tend until they hatch out. A relatively deep tank furnished with suitable plants and smooth surfaces will therefore make them feel at home. As little visual disturbance as possible is also desirable. Commercial breeders in the Far East simulate these conditions by putting a pair of Angels in a 40-litre Chinese jar (like an Ali-baba jar) with water hyacinths (*Eichhornia crassipes*) floating on the top. The Angels are quite happy to spawn undisturbed on the sloping walls of the jar.

Zebra Danios, on the other hand, need totally different conditions. These fishes spawn in a shoal and scatter non-adhesive eggs, which they do not tend and usually try to eat! The ideal way to spawn these fishes is in a shoal of several trios of two males to one female. Place these in a tank which is as long as possible, preferably at least 90cm (36in), with water only about 20cm (8in) deep. Cover most of the floor with marble-

Below: *A Discus guarding a clutch of eggs, showing a parental concern typical of Cichlids. These fishes need soft, clean water and great care.*

sized stones about 1cm (0.4in) in diameter and provide a small section at one end or along the back of the tank with a sandy substrate and suitable plants where the fishes can swim and feed.

If the Danios swim naturally as a shoal then the tank is large enough to allow them to behave as they do in the wild. If the free space in the tank is smaller than the natural size of the shoal, the fishes will swim randomly. Unfortunately, many display aquariums 'cramp the style' of such shoaling species. Fishkeepers thus lose the pleasure of seeing their fishes shoal naturally and reduce the likelihood of successful breeding.

Selection and prior treatment

In many cases, selecting fishes for breeding is simply a matter of ensuring that the specimens are of the right sex, that they are properly matched for size and that the right proportion of males to females is available. However, many fishes, such as Cichlids, will only pair with selected partners. With these it is often a good idea to grow up several specimens from young, preferably obtained from different sources, and to observe the fishes carefully until they have made their own selection before moving them to a separate breeding tank.

It is normally necessary to condition fishes before breeding. This

may involve giving them particularly nutritious food, possibly frozen or live food. Take care with live food, however, that you do not introduce undesirable pests and diseases into the aquarium (see page 65).

Separating the fishes before putting them together for spawning is also an accepted part of the conditioning process, although some fishkeepers argue that it is unnatural. It seems to be an effective way of coaxing chasing egglayers, such as Rosy Barbs, into a spawning mood, and is a convenient way of spawning the fishes when you can be sure to be in attendance to see what happens!

Water quality

Fishes that have been domesticated over several generations tend to be more tolerant to the mineral content and pH of aquarium water than freshly imported wild ones. However, many 'domesticated' fishes will not breed in water too far removed in quality from their natural habitat. Sometimes, even if the fishes spawn

Above: *Festivums beginning the spawning ritual common in Cichlids. Such behaviour precedes the actual spawning on a rock or leaf.*

Below: *The female Festivum lays gelatinous eggs on the surface of a broad-leaved plant as the male fertilizes them. Both parents guard.*

successfully, the eggs will not hatch out if the physiological conditions are not right. Spawn is often particularly susceptible to water quality and may not hatch if the pH or other factors do not fall within a certain fairly narrow range. Neon Tetras, for instance, need soft, acid water with a very low mineral content; they will spawn in water which is only moderately soft, but the eggs will not hatch out.

Using a fresh peat filter can sometimes induce fishes to spawn. The pollen grains in peat release hormone-like substances that seem to stimulate spawning. In the wild, some fishes spawn only when the rains come. This can be simulated by adding extra soft water to reduce the mineral content.

Most fishes spawn more readily in water with low levels of nitrate and organic matter. Certainly, baby fishes are very susceptible to contamination and a much higher proportion of the fry can usually be saved by treating the water with a zeolite/active carbon filter to remove contaminants.

Water temperature
Water temperature can be varied to stimulate breeding. Some coldwater fishes, Goldfishes for example, become interested in breeding when the temperature rises to about 17°C (63°F). Conversely, many tropical fishes can be stimulated into breeding by keeping them relatively cool for some time, then raising the temperature again. In some fishes, a sudden drop in temperature of only a degree or two is an effective spur to breeding behaviour. The easiest way of doing this is to add some cold water or even a few ice cubes to the tank. None of these measures are likely to work, however, if the other conditions in the aquarium – particularly the lighting – are not suitable for breeding.

Lighting
It is very difficult to predict with accuracy which aquariums in a fish-room will be good for breeding and which will not. Two tanks side by side can give quite different results. The angle at which light strikes the tank appears to be important. Early morning direct sunlight seems to act as a powerful stimulant for many species, and this can be simulated with strategically placed spotlamps.

Once the spawn has been laid or hatchlings start to appear, strong direct light is best avoided. Livebearers, however, are not so susceptible to over-lighting, since they are mobile enough to look after themselves, particularly if there is sufficient plant protection available. Too much lighting can frequently

Below: *Passing the water through a simple filter filled with fresh peat (weighted with ceramic pieces) may encourage some fishes to spawn.*

Below: *Strength, direction and rhythm of tank illumination can often influence breeding behaviour. Spot lamps can simulate shafts of sunlight.*

cause death in floating breeding traps. If you leave the trap floating directly under the aquarium lights the babies may receive not only too much light but also too much heat; the small volume of water in the trap rapidly overheats and may kill the babies. Anchor the trap away from the lights.

The rhythm of lighting is also important, particularly for fishes which start to breed at first light and for those that care for their young.

Many Cichlids will let the young stray during daylight hours, but will gather them into the nest as darkness approaches. If aquarium lighting and the room lights are suddenly turned off, the parents receive no warning that dusk is approaching and the next

Below: *A Discus with young fishes in close attendance. For a brief period the fry feed on mucus secreted by the parents' skin, then take live food.*

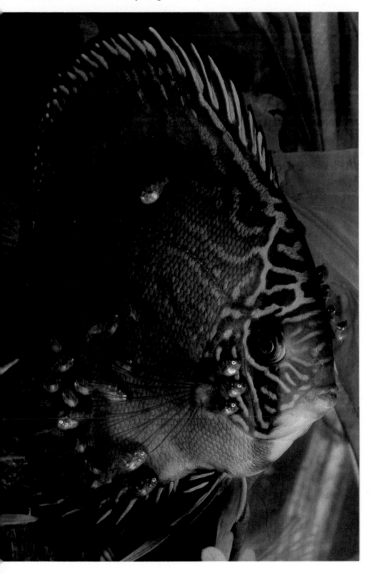

morning they are likely to devour their brood as strangers because they were not cared for overnight. Turning off the main light over the tank some minutes before switching off the room light will give the parents time to gather their brood.

Feeding and aeration
Food requirements for baby fishes vary according to species. Most fishes need a microscopic food to start with; a proprietary liquid fry food is ideal. At this very early stage use very light aeration, both to keep the food particles in suspension and on the move and to keep the aquarium fresh. Secondary powdered foods and, if at all possible, newly hatched brine shrimp can be added to the diet within a few days of the fry becoming free swimming. Increase the aeration gradually as the babies grow bigger, but never sufficiently to run the risk of harming them.

With baby Labyrinth Fishes, it is particularly important to use light aeration after the first week or so to ensure that a film does not develop on the water surface. As the air chamber in the head develops, the babies need to take air from the surface; an oily film will cause them to suffocate.

As baby fishes grow, give them slightly larger brine shrimp, which are easily grown on, and then wean them onto other foods.

Pests and diseases
Eggs and baby fishes are particularly susceptible to attack by pests and diseases that may cause little harm to adults. Snails and planarians (free-living flatworms) can have a feast in a breeding tank, for example. Be sure to eliminate snails from the tank before introducing prospective parents. Planarians are less likely to cause the wholesale damage expected from snails, but they do represent a serious threat and cause some alarm when they emerge from the sand as the fry are being fed. They are much more difficult to eliminate than snails. (See page 69 for suggested methods of eliminating both snails and planarians).

Fishes that care for their young will remove infertile spawn from the mass

These photographs show the early development of a Bristle-nosed Catfish. At 3 days old (above) the young fish is pale in colour and still absorbing the contents of the yolk sac. At 6 days old (below) the sac is gone and the coloration approaches the darker shades of the adult.

of eggs. However, in the absence of parents or when they are not very diligent, infertile eggs quickly become covered in fungus and this can spread to the fertile spawn. Some breeders advocate adding a few drops of methylene blue to the spawning tank; others may add 1 in 10,000 parts of phenoxyethanol or a suitable antibiotic.

Hydra are a much more serious threat to both young egglayers and livebearers. These tiny animals – related to jellyfishes – catch babies in their sting-laden tentacles and digest them in their hollow bodies. Always take great care to exclude *Hydra* from any breeding tank (see page 67).

Many of the parasites that might cause problems during breeding are best eliminated by treating the fishes before they are brought together for spawning. Chief among these parasites are *Oodinium* (a single-celled organism that causes coral fish disease and velvet disease) and gill

flukes (worm-like creatures that cling onto and damage the gills). Both these parasites may live on adult fishes, sometimes keeping a low profile and causing little harm or inconvenience. *Oodinium* is particularly prevalent on Labyrinth Fishes, such as Gouramies, and on Carps and Barbs, such as White Cloud Mountain Minnows, Zebra Danios and Rosy Barbs. Gill flukes are found primarily on coldwater fishes, such as Goldfishes and Koi. In all cases, infestation can wipe out whole broods of fry 7-14 days after hatching unless action is taken.

Above: *A few drops of methylene blue added to the aquarium water provides these Angelfish eggs with some protection against fungi.*

A general policy is to treat all breeding fishes irrespective of possibility of disease, or to breed the fishes once to check if the diseases are present in their dormant condition as a potential threat.

Below: *The thin threads of fungal growth are evident on the infertile eggs in this spawn. Protect fertile eggs by removing the affected ones.*

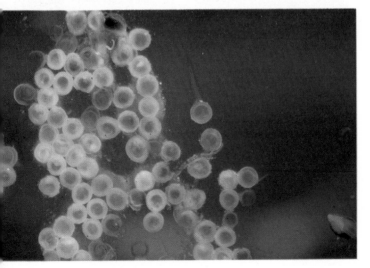

Avoiding Diseases and Reducing Stress

Experienced fishkeepers hardly ever seem to encounter major disease problems, while some beginners reel from one crisis to another. Why should this be so? There are several reasons for this wide disparity in fishkeeping fortunes.

Top of the list must come the supply of fishes in the first place. Experienced fishkeepers develop a special relationship with one or more dealers, whom they know to be particularly careful in selecting and conditioning the fishes they sell. Most fishes sold in aquarist shops are either imported directly or acquired through a wholesaler. Many wholesalers are members of Ornamental Fish International (OFI), a commercial organisation dedicated to maintaining high standards in the handling of imported fishes. Whether the fishes are wild caught or bred in farms, how they are treated and handled before despatch, during the journey and after their arrival influences their ultimate health. Since the chain may be a long one – from

catcher or breeder to shipper to wholesaler to dealer to customer –
every link must be a dependable one.

Introducing new fishes into the aquarium is a critical phase. Every
precaution must be taken to minimize shock and reduce stress
caused by differences in temperature, water quality and environment. And quarantine measures are essential for new fishes being
introduced into an established aquarium.

A common mistake made by beginners is to overstock the
aquarium. More experienced fishkeepers derive greater satisfaction in displaying fewer fishes in uncrowded conditions.

And finally, experienced fishkeepers keep a regular check on the
aquarium conditions, particularly temperature and water quality.
But routine maintenance and inspection does not mean they are
constantly dosing the aquarium with unnecessary remedies. In
short, they do not regard their fishes as a source of worry!

Before we consider fish diseases in detail and how to treat them we shall look briefly at some ways in which fishkeepers can avoid problems in the first place. These range from basic common sense, such as buying healthy stock from reputable dealers, to the potential hazards of using certain live foods. Often it is a question of minimizing stress that makes fishes more susceptible to disease organisms.

Buying fishes

Always obtain your fishes from a reliable source. Check that the dealer adopts proper quarantine procedures and that all the fishes in the tank look healthy; unwell fishes may 'hang back' from the shoal and be slow to react to a gentle tap on the glass (not approved of by dealers!).

A few fishes are bred locally for sale, but most are transported by air over considerable distances. The ultimate health of the fishes therefore depends to a great extent upon the treatment both before and after shipment. Airlines now have considerable experience in handling fishes, and standards are laid down for transport. The fishes are shipped crowded in plastic bags containing as little water as practicable and these are packed inside a cardboard box or expanded polystyrene container. Various exporters use different treatments before shipment, but it is

important that the fishes are unfed, to minimize fouling of the water. Zeolite granules are often added to the container to prevent the build-up of ammonia, nitrite and nitrate.

The fishes may travel in this way for as much as 36 hours. On arrival, the careful importer of freshwater fishes will gradually replace the water in the bag with fresh water as similar as possible to that in the bag, then gradually acclimatize the fishes to local water over a period of several days. Before buying fishes, therefore, check that this procedure has been properly adopted, that the fishes have been quarantined to allow time for possible diseases to develop and that they have been fed to bring them into good condition. It is better to pay a little more for fishes that have been handled properly than to buy cheap fishes that may not survive the multiple shocks of a long air journey followed by being transferred too rapidly to unfamiliar water, then being caught and transported again!

Once you have chosen your fishes, the dealer usually places them in a plastic bag, probably surrounded by a minimum amount of thermal insulation. Be careful not to overheat or chill them on the way home. More substantial insulated containers are available, or low voltage heating and aeration systems that plug into the car cigar lighter can be used to keep the fishes happy during the journey.

Left: *Tropical fishes packed for transportation by air. A few fishes are sealed in each polythene bag with minimum water and plenty of air. The expanded polystyrene case retains essential warmth for the journey.*

Above: *Commercial fish collectors seining for tropical fishes in a Brazilian river. Such waters are rich in Characins, Livebearers and Catfishes. Their catches are destined for aquariums in the USA and Europe.*

Stocking the aquarium

Getting the aquarium ready to receive the fishes starts well before your journey back from the dealer. When setting up the tank, it is important that a biological balance is reached. Otherwise, ammonia and other harmful by-products of waste material from the fishes will not be eliminated by the 'friendly' bacteria that should develop in the system. Therefore, allow the tank a few days to settle down before adding the fishes. This not only enables you to ensure that the heating, filtration, aeration and lighting systems are working properly, but also allows chlorine and chloramine to disperse from the water as it 'matures'.

When introducing fishes to their new environment, ensure that the temperature and quality of the water are suitable. To avoid thermal shock – even rapid changes of 2°C (4°F) can cause distress – float the bag in the aquarium for up to twenty minutes until the temperature equals that in the tank. Matching the water quality can be a much more tricky task. A fish already kept in soft, acid water, for example, has a high chance of dying if suddenly placed in hard, alkaline water. Even a sudden change from fairly heavily polluted water to fresh water can have a harmful effect.

The answer is to ask the dealer what conditions he would recommend, and if possible to read up as much as possible about the

Above: *Marine fishes awaiting release from their temporary polythene homes. Floating the bags in the aquarium water for about 30 minutes helps to avoid thermal shock.*

species in advance. Most freshwater fishes will survive in tapwater from most major areas in the world, but relatively little trouble spent in providing water of better quality is amply repaid. Some fishes, such as Discus, are arguably only happy in soft, acid water, while others, such as Rift Valley Cichlids, are only at home in hard, alkaline water. Neons, for instance, will live quite well in water of medium hardness, but will not breed successfully except in very soft water. Depending upon the region, tank water can be softened either by mixing with rainwater, or by treating the water with an ion-exchange resin (see page 20).

Transferring water slowly from the aquarium to the plastic bag containing the new fishes, perhaps over a period of about 30 minutes, will help to avoid pH shock. A more 'sophisticated' approach is to use an acclimator, a custom-made device

that floats on the surface and gradually allows tank water to mix with the 'transport' water. Also, be sure to ask the dealer if freshwater fishes have been kept in water with a little added salt; this could be a wise precaution anyway for most fishes.

The fishes will feel more at home if hiding places among rocks and plants, even plastic plants, can be provided. The type of plant may be important. For instance, it is clear from the pattern on Angelfishes that they are likely to feel most at home among long-leaved plants, and they will also appreciate broad-leaved plants to lay their eggs on (see page 52). Always introduce plants and rocks before adding the fishes, and check that they are clean. This is particularly important in breeding tanks. Several products are available for cleaning plants effectively and safely for aquarium use.

Take particular care when introducing fishes to an established aquarium. It is wise to quarantine the fishes in an entirely separate container for between two to six weeks, possibly giving treatment for parasites, depending upon the species. Some aquarists give their fishes a strong salt bath before placing them in the aquarium. This can remove many of the possible external parasites, but may stress the fishes unduly. With experience, however, this can be a wise precaution, particularly with coldwater fishes.

The nervousness shown by some fishes when they are introduced into a new aquarium can be overcome with a little insight into 'fish psychology'. The most effective ploy is to add so-called 'dither fishes' first to make the next batch of newcomers feel immediately at home. The 'dither fishes' can be, say, a small Goldfish added before introducing larger, and potentially more nervous, Goldfishes. And midwater swimmers, such as many Cichlids, seem to settle down if there are already other fishes, such as

Left: *This shoal of Barbs is quite at home among the plastic plants in the aquarium. Always plant and furnish the tank before adding the fishes.*

Characins (e.g. Beacon Fish), and some bottom swimmers, such as Catfishes, in the aquarium.

If there has been any sign of disease in the aquarium previously, then the tank and all the equipment, such as filters, plastic plants and nets, should be sterilized. Household bleach is very good for this purpose provided that everything is very thoroughly washed afterwards.

A final word of advice: never overcrowd the aquarium. A few good specimens will give much more satisfaction than a tank crammed full of miserable and potentially unhealthy fishes.

Aquarium design and position
Ideally, the shape of the aquarium should suit the species of fishes it contains. Fast-swimming shoaling fishes, such as Giant Danios, need a reasonably long tank to allow their energies free rein. Labyrinth Fishes, such as Bettas or Gouramies, on the other hand, will thrive in a fairly deep tank. Always ensure, however, that the surface area of the water is sufficient to support the total number of fishes in the aquarium.

The position of the aquarium is also important. Fishes can be scared by light coloured walls close by, for example, or by moving doors or by a constant stream of people hurrying past. Also, experience shows that diseases such as ich (white spot) have consistently developed in aquariums subject to cold draughts.

Choice of lighting is an important element in aquarium design. Most fishes flourish in relatively dim light, but many plants need bright light to prosper. Although many tropical plants grow well in subdued light they do need at least 10 hours of light per day to flourish. Algae-eating fishes, in particular, enjoy periods of bright light, and turtles need light with a high ultraviolet content to maintain good health. Natural lighting can be useful and has the advantage of being free but it is rarely totally satisfactory. In most circumstances, natural light enters through the sides of the tank, whereas fishes are used to top light in their natural habitats. Indirect natural light is best, since the tank may

overheat in a sunny window. When placing a tank in a window, however, take care that draughts are deflected away from it.

Artificial lighting has the advantage that it can be directed from above; top light makes the fishes feel more at home and brings out their colour more fully. The cheapest form of aquarium lights to install are tungsten filament lamps. These provide scarcely adequate light, however, and are relatively expensive to run, may overheat the water and can be dangerous if not properly protected from splashes. Most aquariums are now equipped with flourescent lighting, consisting of one or more tubes and a ballast and starter unit, which may be incorporated in the aquarium hood or placed outside the aquarium. The tubes are connected with special moisture-proof end caps. For safety it is important that the tubes are still protected from

splashing and condensation by some form of transparent cover glass over the top of the water.

Suddenly turning on the lighting may startle the fishes. Some species do not seem to mind, but other more nervous species may be stressed every time the lighting is turned on. This may be particularly disastrous in a breeding tank. One way to overcome this problem is to start by turning on a less bright light, such as a Grolux fluorescent tube that gives out a pinkish light to encourage plant growth, or a tungsten filament lamp. After a short time, the brighter lights can be switched on. Dimmer circuits may also be used for tungsten filament lamps. (See also pages 46-7 and 54-5 for more on lights.)

Potential hazards of live foods
Live foods are a very important source of disease; live *Tubifex* worms are exceptionally guilty in this respect.

Above: *Such a furnished aquarium provides a striking focal point in a living room, but be sure to site it with the fishes' well-being in mind.*

Other live foods, such as *Daphnia*, should be treated with caution. Here we examine some of the most potentially hazardous live foods available to fishkeepers.

Copepods Several species of these tiny crustaceans are used as frozen food, particularly for marine fishes. Many of the free-swimming copepods, such as *Cyclops* (fresh water) and *Calanus* (marine), are harmless in themselves but *Cyclops*, for example, is an intermediate host in the life cycle of certain internal parasitic worms that affect fishes. Other members of the family, such as *Ergasilus, Caligus* and *Lernaea*, are parasitic. All copepods used as food, frozen or dried, ideally should be

Above: A Gammarus *shrimp, a live fish food that may harbour pests, such as the larvae of parasitic worms.*

sterilized by gamma radiation to prevent possible infection being transmitted to the fishes.

Daphnia Water fleas, tiny free-swimming crustaceans that can 'bloom' in tremendous numbers in ponds and rivers during the summer, are a favourite live food for fishes. Unfortunately, they may introduce pests, such as *Hydra*, and sometimes diseases into the aquarium. To avoid problems, always take *Daphnia* from a known reliable source.

Gammarus These so-called freshwater shrimps (they are amphipods and not true shrimps) are relished by larger fishes. If live *Gammarus* are given, then take precautions to avoid the introduction of pests. *Gammarus* may carry the larval forms of nematodes and cestodes (see page 100), parasitic copepods and *Hydra*. Deep frozen *Gammarus* should be irradiated before use; this is normally done during processing.

Below: Tubifex *worms, a popular form of live food for aquarium fishes. They may carry diseases and should be well washed before use.*

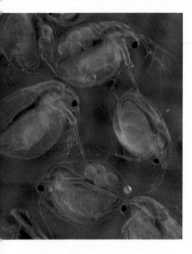

Above: *Water fleas (*Daphnia *sp.) are best collected from a reliable source to avoid introducing pests.*

Tubifex *Tubifex* worms are excellent food for most fishes, and are eagerly eaten, but they are probably the biggest potential source of disease in the aquarium. Some fishkeepers who use *Tubifex* regularly consistently find trouble with various parasites; aquarists who resort to other foods find that their aquariums remain virtually disease free. *Tubifex* – thin, red worms up to 8cm (3.2in) long – are commonly found in large numbers in the mud of polluted waters, such as near sewage outfalls. The front end of the worm sits in a mud tube and the tail waves gently in the water to obtain oxygen. The worms breed very rapidly, laying eggs in oval capsules.

The safest advice is to avoid *Tubifex* worms if your fishes can be tempted to eat any other live food. If you want to use *Tubifex*, then wash the worms gently under running water for several days before use to purge them of as many impurities as possible.

There are several substitutes for *Tubifex* that are completely disease free; white worms and micro-worms, for example, can be cultivated cheaply and easily. Brine shrimps (*Artemia salina*) can be grown to adult size and are ideal as a food for mature fishes. You can also buy them fully grown from your dealer.

Pests in the aquarium
Pests are more likely to be found in ponds than in aquariums, but it is possible to introduce pests into the aquarium by sheer carelessness. Some introduced creatures may be relatively harmless or pose a threat only to fish spawn or fry; others are potentially dangerous to adult fishes. Here is a selection of those most likely to be encountered.

Fish leeches These worm-like parasites attach themselves to the skin of fishes by means of sucking discs at each end of the body. The eggs are laid on water plants and this is the most likely way in which they are introduced into the aquarium or pond. A full description of the problems leeches may cause and the recommended treatments for affected fishes is given in the main disease section of the book (page 90).

Hydra It is difficult to imagine that such a graceful animal could pose any sort of threat in the aquarium. *Hydra* is a freshwater creature related to the corals, sea anemones and jellyfishes. It consists of a hollow extensible tube-like body (basically a digestive cavity) surmounted by between four and ten tentacles surrounding a mouth at one end. There are several species, varying in colour from white to green and brown. The body, when extended, may be 15-25mm (0.6-1in) long, with the tentacles a little shorter.

Hydra can be introduced into the aquarium with live food, such as *Daphnia*, or on plants. In the wild, they are found on the underside of stones or floating leaves. Their normal food is small aquatic crustaceans and worms, but the main concern to fishkeepers is their ability to paralyze and trap baby fishes using the stinging cells on the tentacles.

Hydra can be eliminated by using a copper treatment, a 0.3 percent or 0.5 percent salt solution, or 5mg/l of ammonium nitrate. Removing the fishes and then raising the water temperature to 42°C (108°F) for a few hours is also effective; the plants should not be harmed by this action. Alternatively, use a modern anti-

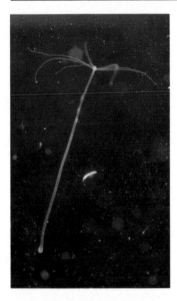

Ostracods Sometimes fishkeepers are concerned by the presence of small bean-shaped organisms in the aquarium. These are crustaceans called ostracods and they are entirely harmless, probably even to the smallest fish spawn. They may be introduced with *Daphnia* or other live food, with water plants, or even through the water supply.

Many species of ostracods are widely distributed in fresh waters and in the sea. The animal lives encased in a single opaque shell, which may be yellowish white to brown or sometimes green in colour and 1-3mm (0.04-0.12in) long. Species living among weeds in ponds are usually up to 1.5mm (0.06in) long. The most obvious protrusions from the shell are two antennae and a pair of slender legs, which are withdrawn rapidly if danger threatens.

Ostracods feed mainly on decaying organic matter and can therefore perform a useful function in the aquarium. They lay small clusters of orange-coloured eggs on water plants in spring, and these can survive in a dried state for many years.

Some fishes will eat ostracods, but unless they become unsightly there is really no need to remove them.

Above: *Although elegant,* Hydra *can paralyze baby fishes with the stinging cells that festoon those extensible tentacles around the mouth.*

parasite treatment. Apparently, Blue Gouramies and Pearl Gouramies will devour *Hydra* if kept reasonably hungry in the aquarium.

Below: *A fish egg that has fallen prey to the attentions of a planarian. These flatworms hide in the sand or gravel during the day and forage for food mainly during the night. They are difficult to clear from the aquarium.*

Planarians These free-living flatworms – known as turbellarians from the vibrating cilia that almost completely cover their bodies – live naturally in both still and running fresh water. They feed on algae and small

creatures and reach a length of up to 30mm (1.2in), depending on the species. Colour varies from greyish white through brown to black.

Planarians are of interest to fishkeepers because they can be introduced with plants and can establish themselves in the sand. They are normally only seen at night, when they scour the walls of the aquarium for food. Although they are harmless to adult fishes, they can destroy large numbers of eggs and fry in a breeding tank.

Planarians can be quite difficult to eliminate. Hanging a piece of fresh meat or liver in the corner of the aquarium in the evening may attract the worms, which can be removed together with the meat the next morning. Modern anti-parasite treatments may be effective. Some fishes, notably Bettas and Gouramies, may eat planarians.

Snails Many snails perform a useful function in the aquarium by rasping at algae growths. This can be particularly useful in destroying growths of blue-green algae, which can choke all the plants and eventually poison the tank. Other snails, such as the Sand Snail (*Melanoides tuberculata*) help to keep the sand in good condition by burrowing into it.

Most snails feed on rotting vegetation and surplus food, but they may turn their attention to your prize aquarium plants! There are some more serious disadvantages in harbouring snails in your aquarium, however. The Wandering Snail (*Lymnaea ovata peregra*), for example, produces a poisonous substance that may cause convulsions in fishes. Fortunately, this species is unlikely to be introduced with cultivated plants. Other species of pond snail act as hosts to the larval stages of internal parasitic worms that infest fishes. However, the most common problem with snails is their appetite for fish spawn; they should be removed from spawning tanks.

Excess snails (except *Lymnaea ovata peregra*!) can be removed by crushing them in the tank, so providing tasty morsels for the fishes. Some fishes, such as Goldfishes and Three-spot Gouramies, will actually suck snails from their shells. Snails can also be removed chemically using a commercial snail-control solution, although it is not advisable to use this on burrowing snails since snails dying in the gravel can pollute the tank. Another effective method is to place a small piece of meat in a glass jar and to remove the snails attracted to the trap. After a few days of such tactics the snail population should be virtually nil.

Below: *This Ramshorn Snail (*Planorbis sp.*) poses no threat in the aquarium, certainly not to the adult fishes. Some snails, however, will devour fish spawn and should be excluded from all breeding tanks.*

Below: *This table summarizes the range of chemicals commonly used to tackle pests and diseases in fishes. Depending upon local regulations, many of these drugs may be available only through a veterinarian, who will be able to provide detailed advice on dosage. The notes in the table are offered only as an approximate guide. Internationally accepted chemical names (instead of trade names) are used here so that a pharmacist or veterinarian in any country will be able to trace the chemical.*

USE OR DESCRIPTION	CHEMICAL	CONCENTRATION
Antibacterial in food	Oxolinic acid	10mg per kg of fish
	Phenoxyethanol	1 percent (10gm/litre)
Antibacterial compounds. Fungicidal and bacterial bath	Benzalkonium chloride	1-4 mg/litre
	Nifurpirinol	1-4 mg/litre
		0.25 mg/litre
	Parachlorophenoxyethanol	20 mg/litre
	Phenoxyethanol	100 mg/litre
Antibiotics	Chloramphenicol	20-50 mg/litre
	Oxytetracycline	13-120 mg/litre
Anti-protozoan	Metronidazole Dimetridazole	1 percent of diet
		4 mg/litre
Anti-TB drugs	Doxycycline Minocycline	2-3 mg/litre as bath
Against intestinal worms	Praziquantel	—
	Levamisole	10 mg/litre for 12-24 hours
Against lymphocystis	Acrinol	—
	Triamcinolone acetonide	—
Various	Methylene blue	2 mg/litre
	Malachite green	Up to 4 mg/litre

In the main disease section of the book the general policy is to recommend the appropriate commercial preparation specially formulated for aquarium use. Most products from major manufacturers are now quite sophisticated.

OTHER DETAILS

Commercial preparation. Used for ulcers etc.

Food soaked in 1 percent solution for specific treatment

Bath for 1 hour

Bath for 1 hour

Continuous bath

Continuous bath

Continuous bath

Used in food or as water treatment.

Hard water reduces effectiveness of oxytetracycline.

Every 12 hours for 3 days in food for intestinal flagellated protozoa.

Bath for 1 hour, for 3-5 consecutive days for flagellated protozoa

Or add to dry food (0.5 mg per gm of food).

Refer to veterinarian for details of use.

Test dose first. Individual fish species may show sensitivity.

Apply as 1 percent solution or ointment

Apply as 1 percent ointment

Traditional treatment for many diseases. Now superseded by more convenient products

Treatment for fungus, parasites etc.

Below: *This table shows the size groups of common pests and diseases affecting fishes. Measurements refer to the maximum dimension in mm and in microns (1/1000mm). Viruses can be seen only with an electron microscope.*

VISIBLE WITH THE NAKED EYE

100mm down to 10mm
Parasitic worms – A few mm to several metres
Fish leech: 30mm
Anchor worm: 20mm
Fish lice: 12mm

10mm down to 1mm
Black spot (Larval trematode): 1-2mm
Copepods (e.g. Ergasilus): 1-2mm
Ich/White spot (Protozoan): 0.2-1mm
Cryptocaryon (Protozoan): 0.2-1mm

VISIBLE WITH A MAGNIFYING GLASS (×10)

1mm down to 0.1mm
Gill flukes (e.g. *Dactylogyrus* sp.): 1mm
Skin flukes (e.g. *Gyrodactylus* sp.): 0.8mm
Ich/White spot (Protozoan): 0.2mm-1mm
Cryptocaryon (Protozoan): 0.2-1mm

VISIBLE WITH LOW-POWER MICROSCOPE (×40-100)

One micron = 1/1000mm
Coral fish disease/Velvet (Protozoan): 15-150 microns
Neon disease (Protozoan): 50 microns
Chilodonella (Protozoan): 40-60 microns
Blood flagellates (Protozoan):
  Body 10-30 microns
  Flagellae 15 microns
Costia (Protozoan):
  Body 10-20 microns
  Flagellae 9-18 microns
Hexamita (Protozoan): 7-12 microns

VISIBLE WITH HIGH-POWER MICROSCOPE (×400-1000)

Fungi (e.g. *Saprolegnia* sp., Ichthyosoporidium): Fungal threads about 2 microns in diameter
Bacteria (e.g. Columnaris, false Neon disease, *Aeromonas* sp., *Mycobacterium* sp.): 2-12 microns

Looking for disease

The first signs of disease are usually obvious to the keen fishkeeper: the fishes will look generally miserable and listless, possibly with folded fins and a whitish hue to the skin. When any of these signs are present, the time has come to examine the fishes more closely.

In this book, the symptoms described are usually those that can be seen with the naked eye, perhaps aided by a magnifying glass. While this may not always enable a precise diagnosis to be reached, it does make it possible to narrow down the

USING COMMON SALT (see p 74

USE
General aquarium additive – mild nitrite protection
Preventative and general nitrite protection
Supportive for coldwater fish with ulcers etc.
Short-term salt dip

APPROXIMATE CAPACITY OF AQUARIUMS

Width Inches (cm)	10" (25)	12" (30)			15" (38)		
Height Inches (cm)	10" (25)	12" (30)	15" (38)	18" (46)	12" (30)	15" (38)	18" (46)
Length Inches (cm)							
12" (30) Imp. galls	3.7	5.5	6.8	8.1	6.9	8.9	10.3
U.S. galls	4.4	6.6	8.2	9.7	8.3	10.7	12.4
Litres	16.8	25.0	30.9	36.8	31.4	40.5	46.8
18" (36) Imp. galls	5.6	8.3	10.3	12.3	10.4	13.4	15.6
U.S. galls	6.7	10.0	12.4	14.8	12.5	16.1	18.7
Litres	25.5	37.7	46.8	55.9	47.3	60.9	70.9
24" (67) Imp. galls	7.5	11.1	13.8	16.4	13.9	17.9	20.8
U.S. galls	9.0	13.3	16.6	19.7	16.7	21.5	25.0
Litres	34.1	50.5	62.7	74.6	63.2	81.4	94.6
30" (76) Imp. galls	9.4	13.6	17.6	20.4	17.3	22.3	26.1
U.S. galls	11.3	16.3	21.1	24.5	20.8	26.8	31.3
Litres	42.7	61.8	80.0	92.7	78.6	101.4	118.7
36" (91) Imp. galls	11.3	16.3	21.1	24.6	20.8	26.8	31.3
U.S. galls	13.6	19.6	25.3	29.5	25.0	32.1	37.6
Litres	51.4	74.1	95.9	111.8	94.6	121.8	142.3
39" (99) Imp. galls	12.3	17.7	22.9	26.6	22.6	29.0	34.0
U.S. galls	14.8	21.2	27.5	31.9	27.1	34.8	40.8
Litres	55.9	80.5	104.1	120.9	102.7	131.8	154.6
48"(122) Imp. galls	15.2	21.8	28.2	32.9	27.9	35.8	41.2
U.S. galls	18.2	26.2	33.8	39.5	33.5	43.0	49.4
Litres	69.1	99.1	128.2	149.6	126.8	162.7	187.3
60"(152) Imp. galls	19.0	27.3	35.4	41.2	34.9	44.9	51.7
U.S. galls	22.8	32.8	42.5	49.4	41.9	53.9	62.0
Litres	86.4	124.1	160.9	187.3	158.7	204.1	235.0

Recommended strength	Grams per litre	Per Imperial gallon		Per US gallon	
		Ounces	Level teaspoons	Ounces	Level teaspoons
0.1 percent	1 gm	0.16	1	0.13	¾
0.3 percent	3 gm	0.48	2¾	0.4	2½
1.0 percent	10 gm	1.6	9	1.3	7½
3.0 percent	30 gm	4.8	27	4.0	22½

Above: *Humble common salt is one of the most effective all-purpose chemicals at the fishkeeper's disposal. In the freshwater aquarium, as the table shows, its uses range from a general additive at low concentrations to a curative bath for some diseases at high concentrations.*

	18″ (46)				
24″ (61)	12″ (30)	15″ (38)	18″ (46)	24″ (61)	30″ (76)
13.7	8.2	10.4	12.5	16.6	19.9
16.4	9.8	12.5	15.0	19.9	23.9
62.3	37.3	47.3	56.8	75.5	90.5
20.7	12.4	15.7	18.8	25.1	30.3
24.8	14.9	18.8	22.6	30.1	36.4
94.1	56.4	71.4	85.5	114.1	137.7
27.7	16.5	21.0	25.2	33.6	40.7
33.2	19.8	25.2	30.2	40.3	48.8
125.9	75.0	95.5	114.6	152.7	185.0
34.6	20.7	26.4	31.6	42.1	50.6
41.5	24.8	31.7	38.0	50.5	60.8
157.3	94.1	120.0	143.7	191.4	230.0
41.6	24.9	31.7	37.9	50.1	61.0
49.9	29.9	38.0	45.5	60.1	73.2
189.1	113.2	144.1	172.3	227.8	277.3
45.1	27.0	34.3	41.1	54.8	66.2
54.1	32.4	41.2	49.3	65.8	79.4
205.0	122.7	155.9	186.8	249.1	300.9
54.7	33.0	42.1	49.8	66.5	81.3
65.6	39.6	50.5	59.8	79.8	97.6
248.7	150.0	191.4	226.4	302.3	369.6
68.7	42.3	52.7	65.6	83.4	102.1
82.4	50.8	63.2	78.7	100.1	122.5
312.3	192.3	239.6	298.2	379.1	464.1

Left: *This table shows the approximate water capacity of aquariums of different sizes. Allowance has been made for the thickness of the glass and for a water level 2.5cm (1in) below the top. To use it, first find your aquarium width in the top section and then the approximate height in the section below it. Follow the selected height column down and read off the aquarium capacity where it coincides with the length of your aquarium. These capacities can be used to calculate heating requirements but make allowance for gravel and furnishings when estimating medicines.*

possible causes sufficiently to render the correct treatment. A more detailed diagnosis may be obtained either by studying one of the specialist books recommended in the reading list, or by sending the body away for post-mortem. However, as you will see below, there are problems associated with post-mortems and the technique is not for the squeamish.

Dead fishes degenerate too rapidly at tropical temperatures for a proper examination to be made. Furthermore, some parasites will leave a dead fish quite quickly. Therefore, dying fishes should be decapitated and kept cool. Samples may be sent to a laboratory for post-mortem wrapped in water-moistened tissue in plastic bags, but a very rapid transport system is necessary. Preferably the affected organs should be preserved in a 4 percent solution of formaldehyde (i.e. a 10 percent formalin solution – since formalin as available from a pharmacy contains 40 percent formaldehyde). At no time should the sample be frozen.

Humane disposal of fishes
Sometimes it becomes obvious that a fish has no chance of survival and that it will be least distressing to the fish and to the fishkeeper to dispose of the unfortunate animal with as little pain as possible. Traditional, rather draconian, methods are either to chop off the head or to place the fish in a net and bring it down sharply on a hard object. However, a more acceptable method may be to place the fish into a dish of ice cubes and then put the dish into the deep freeze.

Using disease remedies
No remedy should be used indiscriminately without first looking for the cause of the disease. Sometimes a disease will return time and time again because this simple exercise is not carried out. One example is the continued recurrence of disease caused by feeding unclean *Tubifex* worms to fishes. Another, less obvious, one is the unaerated aquarium in which fishes always develop ich (white spot); it usually transpires that a cold area in the

aquarium, caused by a draught, is continually stressing the fishes.

With the sophisticated products available today, most fishkeepers are able to use specific remedies prepared by reputable manufacturers rather than going to the trouble of making up their own brew. Always follow the manufacturer's instructions when treating sick fishes. Do not mix remedies without referring to the manufacturer concerned, since some products for two different purposes may contain some common ingredients and the total concentration of these may become too high. Also, two different ingredients may act together to form a toxic combination.

Conversely, however, some chemicals can act together in a beneficial way; a small quantity of salt added to the water, for example, can enhance the effect of some treatments. A similar effect occurs with methylene blue. On its own, methylene blue is an old-fashioned remedy which is not very effective and is inconvenient to use because in any useful concentration it colours the water so deeply that its therapeutic effects become obscured. However, when used in conjunction with other treatments – so that only a faint blue colouration is visible – it has a marked enhancing effect. It has been shown to inhibit the function of undergravel filters, however, for up to three weeks and this can cause problems in a heavily stocked tank.

Common salt (NaCl) must be the most useful chemical for the fishkeeper. Most freshwater fishes and some plants prefer to have a small quantity of salt in the water. It is not clear how this helps to fend off diseases in fishes, but it appears that sodium chloride reduces the immediate effect of nitrite on the fishes. Many livebearers, in particular, definitely flourish with some salt in the water. Some tonic salts also contain additives, such as potassium and calcium, to improve their performance in the aquarium.

Right: *This simplified diagnostic guide relates visible symptoms with possible pests and diseases.*

IDENTIFYING POSSIBLE DISEASES

SIGNS   Numbers refer to the key of possible diseases.

ABNORMAL BEHAVIOUR

Breathing difficulties **19, 33**
Distress/off-colour **5**
Fins closed **10, 21**
Increased respiration rate **4, 10**
Listless/swims abnormally **3, 18**
Loss of appetite/loss of colour **18**
Loss of balance/unable to rise from bottom **30**
Rapid gill movement **8, 19**
Restlessness **15**
Rubbing against hard objects **4, 8, 9, 10, 15, 21, 29, 33**
Swimming awkwardly **9, 22**
Swimming erratically **26**
Swims unevenly/loss of appetite **20**
Whirling motion **27**

LUMPS, SPOTS AND WORMS

Black spots/yellow spots **2**
Disc-like parasites attached to body and fins **16**
Lumps – various shapes **27, 31**
Reddish or white spots merging into patches **17**
Small greyish/white nodules **10, 22**
Small white spots **17, 21, 27**
Small worms on body **29**
Small worms around gills **19**
White to red nodules/very slow growths **25**
Worm-like protruberances **1, 15**

ABNORMAL APPEARANCE
(Except lumps, spots and worms)

Cotton-wool like growths **14**
Curvature of spine **24**
Emaciated **20, 22, 24, 26, 33**
Emaciated/bulbous eyes/skin defects **18**
Emaciated/sunken eyes/pale gills **3, 7**
Eyes become clouded **5**
Fine white threads **6**
Fin edges frayed **13**
Fin edges slightly opaque **13**
Fin membrane breaking up **13**
Fin rays disintegrate **13**
Fins frayed **6**
Flesh eaten away **6, 20, 26**
Gills gaping **19**
Greyish white film, mainly on head **6**
Holes in head **20**
Inflamed gills **8**
Inflamed patches **9, 10, 29**
Inflammation of skin **33**
Intensification of colour **20**
Pine cone appearance due to scales sticking out **11**
Protruding eyes **11, 28**
Reddish coloration in patches or over whole body **23**
Retarded growth **24**
Skin falling away (advanced stages) **4**
Spreading whitish patches **12, 26**
Swollen abdomen **11, 22, 24**
Sunken eyes **11**
Ulcerated body **6, 11, 32**
Whitish opaqueness **4, 8, 9, 29**
Yellow-brown to greyish haze **33**

KEY TO POSSIBLE DISEASES

1 Anchor worms
2 Black spot/Yellow grub (Clinostomum)
3 Blood flagellates
4 Chilodonella
5 Cloudy eye
6 Columnaris
7 Copepods (causing gill infestation)
8 Coral fish disease
9 Costia
10 Cryptocaryon
11 Dropsy
12 False neon disease
13 Finrot/Tailrot
14 Fish fungus
15 Fish leech
16 Fish lice
17 Fish pox
18 Fish TB
19 Gill flukes
20 Hexamita
21 Ich (White spot)
22 Ichthyosporidium
23 Inflammation
24 Internal parasitic worms
25 Lymphocystis
26 Neon disease
27 Nodular diseases
28 Pop-eye
29 Skin flukes
30 Swimbladder trouble
31 Tumours
32 Ulcer disease
33 Velvet disease

An A-Z of Common Pests and Diseases

With a little experience, a glance is usually enough to tell that a fish is ill. A change in behaviour and a general 'unhappy' look are sure signs that trouble is brewing. Unfortunately, many fishkeepers do not notice these first signs and may fail to recognize diseases even when they take a firm hold on the victim. Some diseases, such as ich (white spot), are normally very obvious, but others, such as costia or infestations by gill flukes, may go unnoticed for a long period. Spotting parasites, for example, may need close examination from an unusual angle with extra light and the help of a magnifying glass.

Often, it is the aquarium rather than the fishes that provides early evidence of disorders. In general, the aquarium should not have an excessive amount of dirt. But even the texture of the dirt is important, for some fishes prefer an aquarium which is not entirely clean. However, black patches of sand or decaying food are definite

harbingers of trouble. And if the water has a yellowish coloration, it is almost certainly a sign that the aquarium contains an excess of waste products and that a water change is long overdue. This change, however, must be made gradually to avoid stressing the fishes. Unsuccessful plant growth does not necessarily mean an unhealthy aquarium, but flourishing plants are usually an active indicator that the aquarium is in fine form. Many diseases can lie dormant until conditions in the aquarium deteriorate to a point where the fishes become vulnerable to infection.

This section assumes no special scientific knowledge on the part of the fishkeeper and that a good magnifying glass is the most sophisticated examination technique available. There are a few photographs of microscopic slides, however, to show the structure of some disease organisms in more detail. Idealized life cycle diagrams are included where appropriate, mainly for parasites.

ANCHOR WORM
(Lernaea sp.)
Signs of infection
Female anchor worms – which are the parasites – are easily recognized by their worm-like appearance as they cling on to the fish's body. They reach a maximum length of about 20mm (0.8in) in the spring, when two egg sacs about 3mm (0.1in) form at the free end of the body.

Fishes affected
Anchor worms usually affect fishes in ponds rather than in aquariums. Goldfish, Carp, Orfe and other Cyprinids may be infested by *Lernaea cyprinacaea* and Minnows by *Lernaea phoxinacaea*. Various tropical Cichlids may also be affected by anchor worm.

Details of infection
Despite their common name, anchor worms are not worms at all but tiny crustaceans called copepods. Like most crustaceans, they pass through several larval stages as they mature. The first larvae to hatch from the eggs

Below: *Anchor worms are clearly visible clinging to the skin of this Goldfish. These are the adult females, produced after a cycle involving several larval stages.*

in spring swim freely until they find a suitable host fish and attach themselves to the gill. Once attached they enter a non-swimming stage. The males of the brood fertilize the females and cease being parasitic. The mated females then re-attach themselves to a host fish and develop into the familiar worm-like parasites.

The females shed their eggs in the spring. After this they may die or go on to produce several sets of eggs. As the parasites die, the openings left in the skin and muscles may allow secondary infection from which the fishes may not recover.

Recommended treatment
Anchor worms are firmly attached to the fish, often penetrating deep into the body tissues. The adult 'worms' can be picked off individually and the wound cleaned with a strong solution of potassium permanganate on a small paintbrush, but this is a lengthy process and potentially hazardous to the fish. It is best to use one of the modern anti-parasite treatments in the water to kill the larvae.

The deep wounds left when the parasites are removed may be slow to heal. Help the fishes to recover by keeping them in a fungicidal and bactericidal bath until the wounds heal over completely.

Above: *Black spot on a Dace. The spots are the encysted larvae of a trematode fluke embedded just beneath the skin. Not generally harmful to affected fishes in mild cases and easy to treat.*

BLACK SPOT DISEASE
(Neodiplostomum cuticola – also known as Posthodiplostomum – and other species)
Signs of infection
Small black or brown spots, up to 2mm (0.08in) across, appear on the body and fins, sometimes also on the eyes and mouth.

Fishes affected
Coldwater fishes such as Goldfish, Carp, Tench, and other Cyprinids. Similar conditions, such as yellow grub (*Clinostomum* sp.), affect various tropical fishes.

Details of infection
The spots are heavily pigmented cysts containing the larval stage of a trematode intestinal fluke, such as *Neodiplostomum cuticola*. (The larval stage is also known as *Neascus cuticola*). The adult stage of the worm lives in the intestine of water birds, which become infested by eating fish harbouring the larvae. In the birds' gut the membrane around each larva dissolves and the worm grows to

Below: *A Gold-rimmed Tang with signs of black spot. Such mild infections rarely cause problems and the condition is not directly infectious. Use an anti-parasite treatment.*

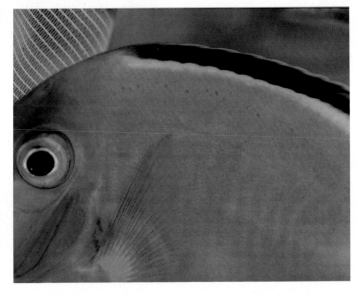

maturity in a period of a few weeks. Eggs produced by the adults pass out in the birds' droppings and those that fall in water develop into free-swimming larvae that infest water snails. Several weeks later the parasites leave the snails and start the cycle again by infesting suitable fish hosts. When the parasites reach about 1mm (0.04in) across a black membrane develops around each one, producing the characteristic spots just beneath the skin.

Mild infections of black spot do little harm to fishes and, because of the complex life cycle, the condition is not infectious from one fish to another.

Recommended treatment
Modern anti-parasite treatments should kill the parasite, although the black spots, once formed, may remain. The most effective preventative action is to break the life cycle of the parasite by ensuring that water birds do not approach the pond or aquarium and that no infected snails are present.

BLOOD FLAGELLATES – SLEEPING SICKNESS
(Cryptobia sp. – which also now includes Trypanoplasma *– and* Trypanosoma *sp.)*
Signs of infection
Fish infected with *Cryptobia* are listless and swim abnormally. They become emaciated, with sunken eyes and pale gills (indicating a lack of red blood cells). Severely affected fishes die. *Trypanosoma* appears to be relatively non-pathogenic and does not produce such drastic symptoms.

Fishes affected
Cryptobia salmositica is found in Cyprinids such as Carp, Goldfish and Tench. *Trypanosoma* species are found in a wide variety of fishes, both marine and freshwater. Aquarium fishes are rarely affected.

Details of infection
Both *Cryptobia* and *Trypanosoma* are single-celled organisms (protozoans) with hair-like flagellae – hence the term 'flagellates' – that live as parasites in the blood. The

dangerous *Cryptobia* has two flagellae, while the virtually harmless *Trypanosoma* has only one. A microscope of at least 300 × magnification is necessary to see these parasites in a blood smear. Both parasites are transmitted by a secondary host – the leech. The flagellates live harmlessly in the leech's intestines and are passed to the fish when the leech bites.

Recommended treatment
No chemical treatment has been found effective against blood flagellates in ornamental fish. Since only fishes which have been attacked by leeches become infected, it is simply necessary to remove infected fishes and eliminate leeches. While this is fairly easy to carry out in aquariums, it is more difficult to tackle the problem in infected ponds.

Below: *The whitish coating on the back of this Spiny Boxfish is a classic symptom of infection by the single-celled ciliate* Chilodonella *sp.*

CHILODONELLA
(Chilodonella sp.)
Signs of infection
Affected fishes rub against hard objects and hold in their fins. A whitish blue opaqueness covers the skin, particularly between the head and the dorsal fin. If the gills are affected, the respiration rate increases noticeably. In the later stages of infection the skin may have a swollen appearance then fall away.

Fishes affected
Chilodonella cyprini is one of the most dangerous and widespread parasites, affecting a wide variety of fishes, particularly if they are injured.

Details of infection
Chilodonella is a ciliate – a single-celled microscopic organism covered unevenly with hairs (cilia) that propel it through the water. It can be seen with a moderate power microscope, but samples must be taken quickly, since *Chilodonella* leaves the fish within two hours of death.

Above: *A Discus with a cloudy eye. Poor water conditions in the aquarium have damaged the eye surface and, in this case, have allowed algae to grow.*

The parasite attacks injured fish first of all, but can spread to healthy fish in crowded conditions. The disease is very debilitating and in severe cases can cause long-standing damage to the gills. Reproduction is by cell division.

Recommended treatment
If the fishes are reasonably strong, an excellent treatment for freshwater species is a 3 percent salt dip; keep the fishes in this until they roll over and then rapidly move them back to their own tank. As an alternative and less stressful treatment use a 1 percent salt solution for 10-15 minutes, then replace the fishes in clean water, preferably at 28-30°C (82-86°F) for tropical species. Otherwise, modern anti-parasite treatments may be used. The parasites will die if left in an aquarium without fishes at 30°C (86°F) for about five days. However, you must still deal with the parasites on the fishes.

CLOUDY EYE
Signs of infection
One or both eyes become clouded over and take on a whitish appearance. Fishes may show signs of distress and be off-colour or they may behave as normal.

Fishes affected
Many fishes can be affected, particularly Cyprinids such as Goldfish, Koi and Barbs; Cichlids such as Angelfish; livebearers such as Mollies and Swordtails.

Details of infection
Cloudy eye can have many causes – look for diseases such as *Oodinium* and *Cryptocaryon*, and also for signs of fish tuberculosis. However, non-specific bacterial infections are frequently the cause.

Recommended treatment
Establish the likely cause of the problem and treat it as quickly as possible to prevent damage to the nervous system. If it is a parasitic infection (such as *Oodinium*), use the treatment shown in the appropriate section. If the cause is bacterial in origin then use a treatment containing an anti-bacterial compound such as phenoxyethanol or nifurpirinol.

The incidence of cloudy eye can be minimized by maintaining good conditions – particularly clean water, since dirty water can be a trigger factor – and by adding a small amount of salt to the water (page 73).

Below: *The blobs of mucus on the tail of this Koi are caused by a type of columnaris. Such bacterial infections spread quickly and need immediate treatment with an antibacterial.*

COLUMNARIS – COTTON WOOL DISEASE
Incorrectly called mouth fungus.
(Flexibacter columnaris – previously known as Chondrococcus columnaris)

Signs of infection
A greyish white film develops over the skin, particularly on the head region, but also on the fins, gills and body. Often, fine white threads are apparent. As the disease progresses, the body may become ulcerated, the fins frayed and the lips and front of the head can be eaten away.

Fishes affected
The disease is very widespread in freshwater fishes, particularly livebearers.

Details of infection
This is a highly contagious disease caused by a bacterium, *Flexibacter columnaris*. Infection spreads through the water and can be transferred by nets and other aquarium equipment. Bacteria enter the fish's body, particularly through wounds and any small abrasions, and multiply rapidly to produce the characteristic symptoms.

Recommended treatment
Columnaris is very virulent and must be treated quickly; fishes affected around the mouth may die within 24 hours. Antibacterial compounds are

effective; use proprietary treatments based on phenoxyethanol, nifurpirinol, benzalkonium chloride, etc. (see pages 70-71).

The best way of avoiding the disease is to keep your fishes in clean, healthy conditions and add a small quantity of salt to the water.

COPEPODS CAUSING GILL INFESTATIONS
(Ergasilus and Caligus sp.)
See also anchor worm, page 78.
Signs of infection
Evidence of infection is very difficult to spot in the early stages. When the parasites really take hold, affected fishes become emaciated and have difficulty in breathing. Raising the gill flap of a dead or anaesthetized fish may reveal the parasites nestling in the gill folds.

Fishes affected
Many species of parasitic copepods – a group within the huge Class of Crustacea – infest the gills of a wide variety of freshwater and marine fishes. The most common parasite is *Ergasilus sieboldi*, which infests many freshwater fishes and has also been reported on herring. This species is

up to 1.7mm (0.067in) long and has a bluish pigmentation. *E. briani* is slightly smaller and also lives on various freshwater fishes. *E. boettgeri* is only up to 0.75mm (0.03in) long and parasitizes tropical freshwater fishes. *E. minor* lacks the blue pigment and parasitizes Tench in particular.

Caligus rapix is commonly found on imported marine aquarium fishes; it affects the skin and fins as well as the gills.

Details of infection
Parasitic copepods take a variety of different forms, of which the anchor worm (*Lernaea* sp.) is probably the extreme.

Copepods that parasitize the gills have a body resembling the well-known non-parasitic copepod, *Cyclops*, which is used as a fish food. The antennae are modified in shape and are prehensile, each ending in a large hook used to penetrate the gill filament of the victim. Only the female is parasitic; the prominent egg sacs are carried at the posterior end of the slender body.

The life cycles of parasitic copepods follow the general pattern of free-living forms, i.e. the eggs hatch into a number of larval stages called nauplii and then into several so-called copepodid stages before developing into the adult form. All the larval stages are free living. In

Below: *Parasitic copepods, such as* Ergasilus sp. *(shown here inset with eggs) can be seen by pulling back the gill flap and using a magnifying glass to confirm identification.*

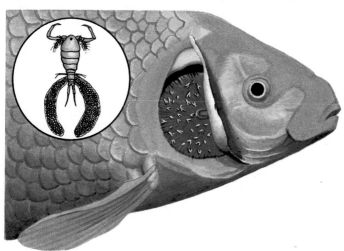

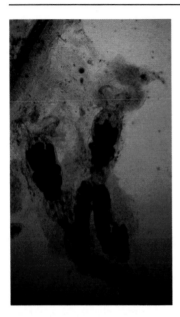

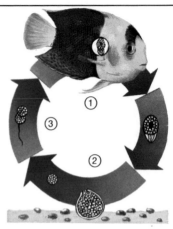

Above: The infection cycle of coral fish disease. 1 The adult fish hosts the parasitic dinoflagellates mainly on the gills. 2 Mature parasites fall off and form cysts. 3 Free-swimming dinospores seek a fresh host.

Above: A microphotograph showing Ergasilus sp. on the gills of a Koi. Such parasitic copepods abound on freshwater fishes in early summer and then again during the autumn.

Ergasilus sieboldi, fairly typical of the parasitic copepods, the adult female is fertilized by the male (which then dies after only about 14 days of life) and then settles on a host as a parasite. Egg sacs develop in spring and the first generation of nauplii is produced in early summer, followed by a larger generation in early autumn.

These copepods may be introduced with live or even non-irradiated deep frozen foods, or with new fishes.

Recommended treatment
Modern anti-parasite treatments are the most successful method of counteracting copepods, since they can be lodged between the gill membranes and may escape complete removal by a salt dip (for freshwater fishes). Apply several treatments at appropriate intervals to ensure complete destruction.

Damaged gills may develop fungus as a secondary infection; treat this in the recommended way.

CORAL FISH DISEASE
(Oodinium ocellatum – also known as Amyloodinium ocellatum)
Signs of infection
The fishes may rub against hard objects, and on close examination there may be some haziness of the skin. The gills may be inflamed; affected fishes typically show rapid gill movements.

Fishes affected
A wide range of marine fishes have been found with this disease.

Details of infection
Oodinium ocellatum is a parasitic single-celled organism called a dinoflagellate. A microscope of 300 × magnification is needed to examine it in detail. O. ocellatum is similar to O. pillularis responsible for freshwater velvet disease (see page 110) but tends to colonize the epithelium of the gills rather more than the body of the fish in the early stages. When the parasites mature they fall to the bottom and form cysts. These break open to release free-swimming dinospores that can live up to 72 hours before attaching to a suitable host fish. This disease is most prevalent in topical marine fishes at 20-25°C (68-77°F).

Recommended treatment

Proprietary remedies containing various copper compounds are very effective – particularly in the absence of coral bed filter media, which will soak up the copper. Unfortunately, copper is particularly toxic to invertebrates. As an alternative, use a modern anti-parasite treatment – but check the instructions carefully because most treatments are harmful to invertebrates, such as sea anemones, corals and crustaceans.

COSTIA

(C. Necatrix, now called Ichthyobodo Necator)

Signs of infection

Affected fishes often swim awkwardly, with their fins folded. They may try to scrape themselves against solid objects. On closer examination, it is possible to see an off-white film over the body, with reddening of the most affected areas.

Fishes affected

Costia is liable to affect freshwater coldwater fishes, and also freshwater tropical fishes kept below 25°C (77°F).

Details of infection

Ichthyobodo (Costia) necator is a microscopic protozoan flagellate, normally with two flagellae. A microscope of 300× magnification is

Below: *The infection cycle of costia.*
1 *The single-celled parasites infect a weakened fish.* 2 *The parasites reproduce by division while attached to the host.* 3 *Cysts formed may lie dormant and then release parasites.*

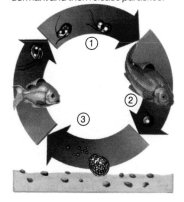

needed to see it clearly. The organism attaches itself to the fish and destroys skin cells, seemingly attacking fishes only when they are weakened in some way and especially when they are overcrowded. In ponds this is particularly likely at the onset of spring, when the fish may be weakened by an excess of waste products in the water or because of an inadequate diet, or because the fishes have just come out of their winter dormancy.

While attached to their host, the parasites reproduce asexually by simple division, two more flagellae being produced just before division. Parasites that fall off the fish normally die within an hour, so the infection only thrives in crowded conditions where hosts are plentiful. However, some cysts are produced and they may lie dormant for a time before releasing a fresh supply of parasites.

When the infestation occurs, fishes are likely to die within a few days if they are not treated.

Recommended treatment

Heat is the simplest form of treatment; *Ichthyobodo* is 'unhappy' at 25°C (77°F) and dies at 30°C (86°F). If it is possible without harming the fishes, raise the temperature of the water to 30°C for a few hours to eliminate the parasites. This may be dangerous, however, if the fishes are suffering a severe infestation of the delicate gill membranes.

Alternative treatments include a 3 percent salt dip until the fishes roll over (then quickly move them back into their own tank), a 1 percent salt bath for 20 minutes or one of the modern anti-parasite preparations. After treatment, transfer the fishes to a clean, sterilized tank with fresh matured water and ensure that they are not overcrowded.

CRYPTOCARYON – SALT WATER ICH

(Cryptocaryon irritans)

Signs of infection

Soon after infection fishes scrape themselves energetically against stones and hold their fins close to the body. As the disease progresses, greyish white nodules about 2mm

(0.08in) in diameter appear on the skin, although these are sometimes obscured by inflamed patches. Respiration becomes rapid if the gills are infested.

Fishes affected
Most marine fishes can be affected by this very common parasite.

Details of infection
Cryptocaryon is closely related to *Ichthyophthirius* that causes ich or white spot (see page 96). It is a ciliate protozoan (i.e. a one-celled organism with many small hairs to propel itself) that penetrates the outer layer of skin and mouth area and causes extreme irritation, resulting in red patches of inflammation. Secondary infection by bacteria, fungi and other parasites may set in.

On maturity, *Cryptocaryon* leaves the fish and subdivides to form many more organisms that re-infect already affected fishes and attack healthy ones in the aquarium.

Below: *A Red Emperor with the whitish nodules caused by the single-celled parasite* Cryptocaryon irritans. *Treatment may be difficult.*

Recommended treatment
This parasite is quite resistant to treatment. Remedies containing copper are effective, but use these with care, especially if there are invertebrates in the aquarium. Alternatively, modern anti-parasite remedies should be effective – but check the instructions carefully because most treatments are harmful to invertebrates. Some of the human antimalarial drugs have been used with success.

DROPSY – ASCITES
(Aeromonas sp. and various other bacteria)
Signs of infection
The belly of the fish becomes distended, sometimes accompanied by ulcers. The eyes may protrude or may be sunken. The scales frequently stick out, giving a 'pine cone' appearance.

Fishes affected
Dropsy affects Cyprinids, such as Carp and Tench, and occasionally freshwater tropical fishes, such as Gouramies – particularly Dwarf Gouramies. Livebearers and Characins may also be affected.

Details of infection
A variety of bacteria – particularly *Aeromonas* sp. – cause dropsy. Viruses can also be associated with the disease.

Due to damage to the heart and blood vessels, blood-stained fluid builds up in the abdomen, and sometimes behind the eye. Ulcers may appear. Affected fishes usually die quite quickly.

Recommended treatment
The disease is encouraged by adverse conditions. Treatment is uncertain, but using foods or baths containing antibacterials such as nifurpirinol can be successful. Prepared food containing oxolinic acid is also worth trying. Baths of parachlorophenoxyethanol have also been reported to be successful and supportive treatment by maintaining fishes in salt baths is also worthwhile. See the chart of chemicals on pages 70-71 for a summary of possible treatments for this condition.

Above: *This close up of a Koi with dropsy shows the typical symptom of lifting scales caused by a build-up of pressure in the abdomen.*

Below: *The 'pine-cone' appearance of protruding scales caused by dropsy is clearly visible in the* Labeo bicolor *in the foreground of this shoal.*

FALSE NEON DISEASE
Signs of infection
The symptoms are similar to those caused by *Pleistophora hyphessobryconis* in neon disease (see page 104), although the spreading patches are paler in colour.

Fishes affected
Characins are mainly affected. When the symptoms of neon disease show, always suspect false neon disease as an alternative.

Details of infection
Little is known about this disease, except that it is caused by bacterial infection. Looking at the symptoms, it is virtually impossible for the aquarist to distinguish between the sporozoan causing neon disease and the bacterial infection described above. Some protozoan skin diseases, such as chilodonella, can also affect Tetras, giving very similar symptoms.

Recommended treatment
Cleanliness in the aquarium is paramount. Successful treatment has been reported using anti-bacterials and remedies containing nifurpirinol.

Below: *Bacterial finrot has caused the membrane between the fin rays of this marine Angel to disintegrate. The damage will spread to the body.*

FINROT/TAILROT
(Aeromonas hydrophila – formerly A. liquefaciens – and other species)
Signs of infection
At first the edges of the fins take on a slightly opaque appearance. Then pieces of the membrane come away, exposing the rays, which in turn begin to disintegrate. Affected fishes normally die when the disintegration reaches the body.

Fin-nipping fishes can cause a similar effect and the damaged fins are then subject to bacterial attack.

Fishes affected

Finrot occurs in many species of freshwater and marine fishes. Long-finned fishes, such as Angelfishes and coldwater Veiltails, are particularly susceptible. The poor circulation in the extended fins of Veiltails, for example, becomes a critical factor when the temperature drops below 10°C (50°F).

Details of infection

The bacteria that cause finrot, particularly *Aeromonas hydrophila*, *Pseudomonas fluorescens* and *Vibrio anguillarium* are probably always present; they only take hold on unhealthy fishes in a poor environment. These bacteria are also responsible for a wide range of symptoms such as spots, inflamed areas and ulcers. The damage caused by bacterial infections makes the affected fishes vulnerable to attack from other disease organisms such as fungi, viruses and parasites.

Recommended treatment

As with so many diseases, unless the conditions are satisfactory, any chemical cure will not be fully effective. There are several proprietary treatments based on phenoxyethanol, para-chloro-phenoxyethanol or nifurpirinol; these may be effective provided treatment

Above: *The tail of this fish has suffered extreme damage as a result of bacterial infection. Fin-nipping causes a similar appearance.*

is not delayed. Bactericidal chemicals such as benzalkonium chloride can also be used. The temperature of the water for coldwater fishes should be raised to at least 16°C (61°F).

FISH FUNGUS – SAPROLEGNIA
(Saprolegnia sp and Achlya sp.)
Signs of infection

The clear signs of infection are cotton-wool-like growths, normally white, but also sometimes greyish black to green. Fungus normally starts on the body but can originate wherever there is some kind of damage. It may spread to affect the fins, mouth, eyes and gills.

Fishes affected

All fishes are potentially vulnerable.

Details of infection

Fungi are plants that live on dead organic matter. Characteristically the fungal body, or mycelium, is made up of very fine filaments, or hyphae, that penetrate dead and decaying tissues and absorb nutrients directly through their cell walls. Thus, healthy fishes will resist infection even though fungal spores are present in the water. The

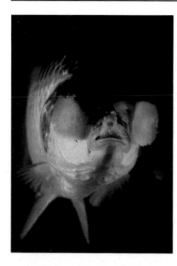

Above: *Fungal infection of the eyes has caused this swelling. If the fungus engulfs the gills, the fish will almost certainly die unless treated.*

spores are released from the swollen tips of certain hyphae and swim freely by means of two flagellae until they alight upon suitable tissues and start to grow into another fungal mass.

Fungus only attacks fishes that have been injured or weakened in some way. If an attack appears to occur spontaneously, it is probably a secondary infection of tissues damaged by another agent, by skin flukes for example. In these cases, both the fungus and the primary infection need treatment. Fungus will kill if not treated.

Damaged or infertile eggs are particularly open to fungal attack, while healthy eggs in the same mass of spawn may hatch normally. It is always wise to remove eggs with fungal growths to safeguard the healthy eggs from any check on their development (see photo on page 57).

Recommended treatment

In aquariums, prevent possible infection by checking that the water is in good condition, at a suitable temperature and not too alkaline (preferably pH 7.2 for freshwater aquariums). Many treatments have been recommended but some of them have serious disadvantages.

Salt baths are a traditional remedy for freshwater fishes, but they may cause undue stress and need frequent changing, and on their own they are not particularly effective. Methylene blue is effective in mild cases, but the strength required colours the water and makes it difficult to keep a check on progress. Malachite green can be painted onto infected areas. Several modern proprietary treatments are available and these are generally effective against fungus.

In ponds, fungus usually occurs in the spring, when the fishes are at their weakest, or after spawning, when they may become damaged. It is possible to reduce the chance of fungal infection by 'fattening' the fishes by feeding well-balanced and nutritious foods (lumps of plain cooked porridge are appreciated as a fattening food) before the onset of wet or cold weather and ensuring that the pH of the water is satisfactory (between pH 6.5 and pH 7.8). There are proprietary fungus treatments designed to be used in ponds. However, depending upon the circumstances, it is better to remove the infected fishes to a suitable container for treatment, where more stable conditons can be maintained; extremes of heat and cold can reduce the effectiveness of medications and encourage further infections. Be sure to transfer the fishes carefully into a large container, an old bath for example, filled with dechlorinated or aged water. Ideally, aerate the water. Avoid undue stress at all costs. While transferring fishes, wipe away the fungal growth with cotton wool.

FISH LEECH

(e.g. Piscicola geometra)
Signs of infection
Affected fishes are very restless and try to remove the parasites by rubbing against hard objects. Closer inspection reveals the worm-like leeches – up to at least 30mm (1.2in) long – clinging to the body.

Fishes affected

Many species may be attacked, particularly the Carp family. Leeches occur frequently in ponds but very seldom in aquariums.

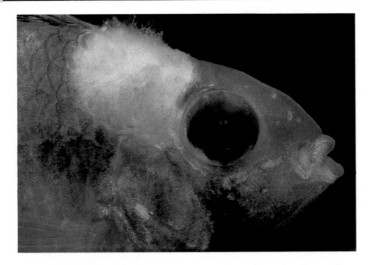

Above: *The white threads of
Saprolegnia fungus protrude from the
skin of this infected fish. Fungus
seems to affect weakened fishes.*

Details of infestation

There are about 300 species of
leeches, mainly from fresh water.
They are worm-like creatures with a
sucking disc at each end of their
segmented bodies. They can move
either by a looping action, extending
and contracting the body and using
the suckers alternately as points of
attachment, or they may swim with

Below: *Fish leeches* (Piscicola
geometra) *on the skin of a Goldfish.
The leeches draw blood from their
host and may pass on infections.*

the same looping action. One sucker
houses a mouth, which can inflict a
wound through which the leech
extracts an amazing quantity of blood
from its host. An anti-clotting agent in
the leech's saliva keeps the blood
flowing freely from the wound.

Leeches are hermaphrodite i.e.
each individual has both male and
female organs, although two leeches
appear to be involved in mating.
Piscicola geometra lays its eggs in
cocoons about 4mm (0.16in) long on
water plants; this is the most likely
way they are transmitted into the
aquarium or pond.

Besides the debilitating effect on
the fishes, leeches are carriers of
blood flagellates such as
Trypanosoma, and the wounds they

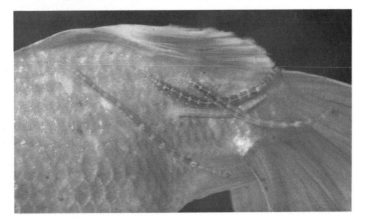

Above: *An individual fish louse (Argulus* sp.), *about 1cm (0.4in) long. The paired feathery legs help to identify it as a crustacean.*

cause can be the source of secondary infections, such as fungus and bacterial septicaemias.

Recommended treatment
A 3 percent salt dip is usually effective in removing leeches. Pull off any leeches that do not fall off during this dip, but to avoid undue damage to the fish do not remove leeches before salt treatment. Some modern anti-parasite treatments will eliminate leeches effectively.

To clear ponds, try hanging a piece of raw meat in a glass jar in the water to attract the leeches. You can then remove and destroy the leeches, although this is a somewhat laborious process to carry out.

FISH LICE
(Argulus sp.)
Signs of infection
Fish lice are disc-shaped parasites between 8 and 12mm (0.3-0.5in) in diameter and varying in colour from light green to brown. They can be seen attached to the body and fins.

Fishes affected
Fish lice may affect many species of coldwater fishes. They are unlikely to be found on tropical species unless the parasite is introduced into the aquarium on live food or plants. Even then the lice may not survive for very long in the warm water conditions.

Below: *A fish louse (Argulus sp.) adhering closely to the skin of a Goldfish by means of its two suckers. It draws blood and tissues from its host through a 'hypodermic' spine.*

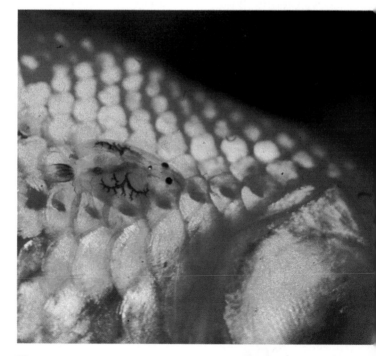

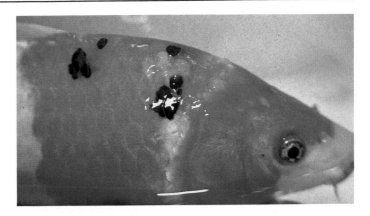

Details of infection

These parasitic crustaceans have eight feathery legs that they use for swimming in search of a host fish. The small tail is used for steering and also contains the reproductive and breathing organs. On the under-surface two powerful suckers enable the fish lice to cling firmly to the host's scales. Between the suckers is a poison spine capable of injecting an anti-clotting agent into the fish and a proboscis associated with it is used to draw off blood and body tissues from beneath the skin.

There are about 200 species of *Argulus* worldwide. The most commonly found are *A. foliaceus, A. coregoni,* and *A. japonicus.*

The eggs are normally laid in midsummer on a stone or other solid surface. The larvae hatch out about a month later and swim freely until they find a host fish. When well fed, they move from fish to fish at will, sometimes not feeding for several days. Five or six weeks after hatching, they are capable of reproduction. Fish lice are suspected of transmitting diseases such as dropsy.

Recommended treatment

Since they are quite large, fish lice can be removed individually from affected fishes using forceps. If necessary, a touch of strong salt solution applied carefully with a paintbrush will help to dislodge them. Alternatively, add a modern anti-parasite treatment to the water. Do this in a hospital tank so that the dislodged parasites can be removed from the environment.

Above: *The hard glistening blobs on this Koi are caused by carp pox, a viral infection that may clear up of its own accord in a few weeks.*

FISH POX/CARP POX – SKIN PAPILLOMA
Signs of infection

This disease manifests itself as small, opalescent white spots with a greasy appearance and possibly with streaks of black pigment, standing proud of the skin by 1 to 2mm (up to 0.08in) and gradually increasing in size. The spots may merge, so that large areas of the skin are affected. The growths are quite firm and, as they age, they may take on a reddish grey appearance.

Fishes affected

This disease appears mainly in Carp, hence the popular name Carp pox. It has also been found in Bream, Perch, Pike, Rudd and Tench, and on various aquarium fishes.

Details of infection

It is thought that fish pox is primarily caused by a species specific virus.

Recommended treatment

There is no known effective chemical treatment for fish pox. If affected fishes are kept in clean, healthy surroundings then the signs should disappear after 8-12 weeks. They may reappear, but are unlikely to do so on really healthy fishes. Previously uninfected fishes introduced into a pond where this has occurred are likely to suffer in the spring.

FISH TUBERCULOSIS
(Mycobacterium and Nocardia sp.)
Signs of infection
The signs can be very varied. Affected fishes can show loss of appetite, become listless and lose their colour. Later in the course of the disease, they may become emaciated and develop bulbous eyes and skin defects. They may also suffer a deformed spine. Frequently, no outward signs are apparent before several fishes die suddenly.

Fishes affected
All aquarium fishes are susceptible to fish TB, particularly Anabantids, Characins and Cyprinids. In the wild, both marine and freshwater fishes are affected, but seldom seriously.

Above: *Skin defects, emaciation and bulbous eyes – typical of fish TB shown by a Marshall Island Wrasse.*

Details of infection
The bacteria responsible for fish TB, *Mycobacterium* and other species, are frequently present in fishes but do not necessarily cause any harm unless conditions are adverse. These bacteria can infect man, so take care not to swallow aquarium water when siphoning and wash your hands thoroughly after servicing your tank.

Below: *A Dwarf Gourami with the early symptoms of fish TB, notably slight emaciation and skin defects. Once advanced, it is difficult to treat.*

Recommended treatment

In the early stages, human anti-TB drugs (consult your veterinarian) may prove effective, but once the disease is advanced it does not seem to respond. Since the bacteria grow most rapidly at 25°C (77°F), raising the temperature of the water is not a recommended treatment. However, the disease can be prevented from taking hold by keeping fishes in good conditions, when their natural resistance seems able to cope.

Always remove sick and dying fish; cannibalism will occur otherwise and this is a sure way of spreading the disease in the aquarium.

Below: *A microphotograph reveals two gill flukes (*Dactylogyrus sp.*) on a fish gill. These trematode parasites are particularly harmful to baby fishes; much less so to adults.*

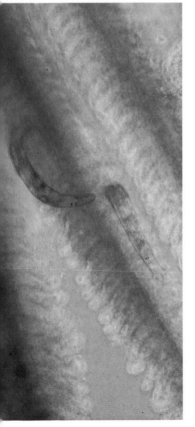

GILL FLUKES
(Dactylogyrus and other species)
Signs of infection

Healthy adult fishes can often host small numbers of gill flukes without any ill effect and these are difficult to spot with the naked eye. Careful study with a good magnifying glass under good light may reveal the flukes on adults or fry, otherwise you will need a microscope to confirm your suspicions. Heavily infected fishes show the characteristic symptoms of increased respiration rate and gaping gills. On newly hatched fry, a whitish mass may be seen around the gills on about the seventh day after hatching.

Fishes affected

Dactylogyrus sp. are found in all species of Cyprinids, and also in other fishes, such as Guppies and Characins. Other related species of gill flukes seem to be common on aquarium fishes, ranging as widely as Angelfishes, Glassfishes and marine Pufferfishes.

Details of infection

Dactylogyrus and the related species are monogenetic trematodes – small, worm-like creatures up to 1mm (0.04in) long – that develop totally within one host. The parasites anchor themselves to the gills by means of an attachment disc with several hooks around the edge and two or four clasping hooks in the centre, depending on the species.

All species reproduce by depositing resistant eggs, which hatch into free-swimming larvae that infect new hosts. The eggs can survive over the winter to produce an infection in the spring.

Generally, healthy fishes can contain an infection. If a fish is out of condition, the infestation may become severe and the parasites spread to the main body areas.

Recommended treatment

Adult fishes may be treated either with a 3 percent salt dip or with a modern anti-parasite remedy. If baby fishes become infected, try adding 15-50mg/l of formalin to the water or use a suitable anti-parasite treatment recommended by your dealer.

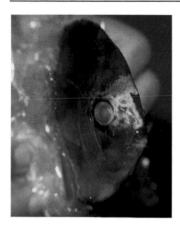

HEXAMITA/SPIRONUCLEUS –
HOLE-IN-THE-HEAD
(Hexamita sp. – formerly Octomitus sp. – and Spironucleus sp.)
Signs of infection
Affected fishes first lose their appetite, then their colour becomes more intense and they begin to swim unevenly. In Discus fishes particularly, and sometimes in other fishes, small holes appear in the head, with the parasites showing as whitish material extending from the holes. The parasites can also be detected in fresh excreta.

As the disease progresses, fishes become emaciated and the holes spread as the flesh is eaten away.

Fishes affected
This disease is most feared in Discus fishes, the so-called 'hole-in-the-head' disease, or Discus disease, which may have other, as yet unidentified, causes. It may appear in the same form particularly in Angelfishes, Gouramies, Goldfishes and even in some marine fishes.

Details of infection
Hexamita sp. and *Spironucleus* sp. are microscopic single-celled parasites with eight flagellae; *Spironucleus* is rather rounder and less elongated in shape than *Hexamita*. Both parasites live in a similar manner, but *Spironucleus* is usually less debilitating.

Very little is known about the reproduction cycle, but in crowded conditions the parasites are probably

Above left: *Severe infestation by* Hexamita *sp. has caused the characteristic 'hole-in-the-head' symptoms in this Discus.*

Above: *The first stages of 'hole-in-the-head' in an Oscar. Such lesions may become the site for fungal or bacterial infections.*

passed on by being taken in with food. They multiply in the intestine and spread via the blood to all internal organs in the body. An affected fish may become emaciated and die without showing any surface damage. This is particularly common in young Cichlids and Gouramies. The craters in Discus and other fishes very quickly succumb to secondary infection by fungi and bacteria.

Recommended treatment
A treatment is available especially to treat *Hexamita*, but some modern anti-parasite compounds are also effective. The disease responds to metronidazole and dimetridazole (a veterinary prescription may be necessary) given via the food and water. Be sure to treat early for success and also tackle the secondary infections with suitable antifungal and antibacterial products

ICH – WHITE SPOT
(Ichthyophthirius multifiliis)
Signs of infection
Infected fishes try to close up their fins and rub against hard objects. The

Above: *White spot infection cycle*
1 Parasites beneath skin. 2 Mature
parasites break through skin and
form capsule. 3 Free-swimming
tomites in search of a new host.

parasites show up as white, pinhead-
size specks on the fins and body.

Ich should not be confused with the
similar white tubercles that appear on
the pectoral fins and gill plates of male
fishes, particularly Goldfishes, at
breeding time.

Fishes affected

Virtually all freshwater aquarium
fishes can be affected. An epidemic is
less likely to occur in acid water.

Details of infection

Ichthyophthirius multifiliis is a single-
celled ciliate parasite that on maturity
reaches 0.2-1mm (0.008-0.04in) in
diameter and has a characteristic
curved nucleus. It rotates constantly
by means of its many cilia.

Fishes are infected by the highly
mobile free-swimming stage of the
parasites. These young parasites (or
tomites) are only up to 0.05mm
(0.002in) long and propel themselves
through the water by beating their
cilia. They must find a suitable host
within two days of being released or
they die. Should they alight on a fish,
they rapidly penetrate the outer skin
layer and live between the skin and
the underlying tissue, feeding on
body fluids and skin cells. They

Below: *The classic symptoms of ich,*
or white spot, on a Waroo or Triangle
Cichlid. This parasitic infection
responds well to treatment by
commercial preparations.

Above: *The glistening white spots caused by the single-celled parasite* Ichthyophthirius sp. *are clearly visible in this freshwater tropical fish.*

remain in the skin and grow for up to three weeks, depending upon the temperature; growth virtually ceases below 10°C (50°F) and is most rapid at tropical temperatures. When mature, the parasites bore through the skin, fall to the bottom of the aquarium and become attached to a solid surface. Here they become enclosed in a gelatinous capsule, or cyst, and start to divide inside. Within 15-20 hours, up to 1000 free-swimming tomites are released into the water to start the cycle all over again in the aquarium.

It is clear that the parasites can attach themselves to a fish and remain dormant until the fish is 'off-colour' or weakened in some way. This probably explains the unexpected outbreaks which sometimes recur.

Recommended treatment

Very effective, specific white spot treatments are available. These normally consist of malachite green mixed with other chemicals to enhance the effect. It is easiest to attack the parasite in the free-swimming stage, but some treatments claim to be effective against the parasites on the body.

A further method of treatment strikes at the need of the free-swimming parasites to find a host within 48 hours of being released from the cysts. The technique consists of transferring the fishes from one tank to another every 12 hours. To be really effective, seven different tanks are necessary. A

variant on this approach is to use a filtration/sterilization system with a powerful flow and a very efficient filter, such as a diatom filter. This prevents the mature parasites settling to form cysts once they have left the affected fish's body.

ICHTHYOSPORIDIUM

(Ichthyosporidium hoferi)
See also fish tuberculosis page 94
Signs of infection

Fishes appear emaciated and yet have swollen abdomens. Skin defects may appear, particularly in the advanced stages of the disease, when small white nodules appear on the skin. Infected fishes swim abnormally.

Fishes affected

Ichthyosporidium affects a wide range of both freshwater and marine fishes. The disease is not as common as it was once thought, due to the confusion with the very similar symptoms caused by fish tuberculosis.

Details of infection

Ichthyosporidium is a fungal disease that spreads throughout the body and severely damages the internal organs. The life cycle is quite complex, infection taking place from spores that are ingested – possibly on copepods taken for food – or which settle on open wounds. Cultures of the fungus raised in the laboratory grow actively at 3-20°C (34-68°F), with optimum growth at 10°C (50°F).

Recommended treatment

If the ichthyosporidium is in an advanced stage, then treatment is unlikely to be successful. However, it may be possible to save fishes that have only just become infected. Food soaked in phenoxyethanol and using baths of parachlorophenoxyethanol have been claimed to be successful; take care not to use the two chemicals in the same tank. Raising the temperature to 38°C (100°F) has been tried but cannot be considered a proven treatment.

If the fishes have to be destroyed, ensure that the aquarium and all the equipment is thoroughly disinfected before re-use (see page 64)

Above: *The infection cycle of ichthyosporidium. 1 Fungal spores liberated from affected fishes may cause infection by settling on open wounds. 2 Copepods ingested as food may also carry the spores.*

INFLAMMATION – BACTERIAL SEPTICAEMIAS

(Aeromonas sp., Pseudomonas sp. and others)

Signs of infection

A reddening on or under the skin over part or the whole of the body. Fishes behave normally at first but can quickly become very poorly and die.

Fishes affected

All fishes are open to infection.

Details of infection

The natural defence mechanism that enables healthy fishes to resist bacterial infection may break down when waste products in the water build up to a high level. Isolated red patches appear on the body and, without treatment, may spread and rapidly kill infected fishes.

Recommended treatment

If the infection is in its early stages then restoring clean conditions may be sufficient to effect a cure. However, using an antibacterial, such as nifurpirinol, or an antibiotic can clear up even quite advanced cases in a very short time.

Below: *Signs of inflammation are evident here. Such bacterial septicaemias need swift treatment to prevent affected fishes dying.*

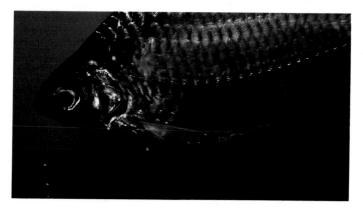

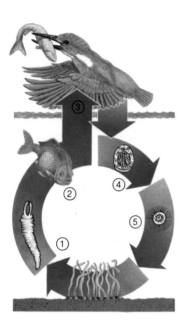

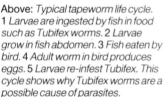

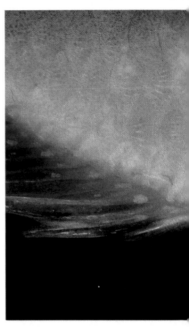

Above: *Typical tapeworm life cycle.*
1 Larvae are ingested by fish in food
such as Tubifex worms. 2 Larvae
grow in fish abdomen. 3 Fish eaten by
bird. 4 Adult worm in bird produces
eggs. 5 Larvae re-infest Tubifex. This
cycle shows why Tubifex worms are a
possible cause of parasites.

INTERNAL PARASITIC WORMS
Signs of infection
One of the first signs may be retarded
growth. Certain species of fish may
become thin, with the body caved in
near the heart but the abdomen
distended. With tapeworm infection,
the abdomen may eventually burst.
Mild infections may be tolerated by
the fishes without the fishkeeper even
being aware of the trouble.

Fishes affected
Intestinal worms are most frequently
found in outdoor fishes. Tropical
aquarium fishes may be infested
either because they are wild caught or
through feeding with certain live foods
that carry the parasites.

Details of infection
The following types of parasitic
worms may be encountered:

Acanthocephala – Thorny headed worms
These parasites (varying in size from a
few millimetres to several
centimetres) attach themselves to the
intestine, frequently damaging the
lining and making the fish vulnerable
to other infections and parasites.
They hang onto the gut lining by
means of a cluster of tiny hooks and
absorb food over their entire body
surface. Eggs produced by the adult
worms are excreted by the fish and
hatch into larvae that live in
crustaceans, such as freshwater
shrimps (*Gammarus* sp.). Since these
are a favourite food for many fishes,
particularly Cichlids, the larvae are
transferred to the intestines, where
they grow into adult worms. Be sure
to discard any *Gammarus* shrimps
that contain red spots; these are the
Acanthocephala larvae.

Cestodes – Tapeworms
Tapeworms are typically flattened
and ribbon-like in shape, and may be
up to several metres long in some
species. They use sucking discs or
hooks, or a combination of both, to
attach themselves to the intestine or
belly (i.e. body cavity) of their host
fishes. Some tapeworms infest the

Above: *Bright red* Camallanus *worms protruding from the anus of an infested fish. These parasites draw blood from the rectum lining.*

belly of one fish as a larva and, after being eaten, the intestine of a larger fish as an adult.

Most tapeworm life cycles involve the production of eggs (sometimes inside discarded segments of the worm) that pass out of the host and develop into larval stages of increasing complexity. The crustacean *Cyclops* and *Tubifex* worms are both potential carriers of tapeworm larvae. There is always a risk in feeding fishes with these live foods, since they are usually collected from water in which fishes live. Some species of tapeworm reach the adult stage in water birds or mammals, infesting fishes only as an intermediate host in the life cycle.

The degree of harm caused to fishes varies from one tapeworm species to another; in general they are very undesirable in aquarium fishes.

Nematodes – Threadworms or roundworms

Nematodes are unsegmented worms that vary in length from less than 1mm to 9m (0.04in-29.5ft). Fishes may be the final hosts or intermediate hosts in the life cycles of various parasitic nematodes. If they harbour the adult worms then these are usually found in the intestine; larval stages generally appear as encapsulated nodules up to 1mm (0.04in) across in the muscles and internal organs. Many parasitic nematodes affect wild fishes, but only a few species are likely to be encountered in aquarium fishes. Notable among these are *Capillaria* and *Camallanus*.

Capillaria may infest Corydoras Catfishes and Cichlids, such as Angelfishes and Discus. The adult worm, between 1-20mm (0.04-0.8in) long depending on species, lives in the intestine. It produces copious supplies of eggs, which are passed out with the faeces and can be recognized under a microscope.

Camallanus, a bright red nematode worm only a few millimetres long, infects the rectum of aquarium fishes, particularly livebearing species such as Guppies and Mollies. It grips the gut lining by means of tiny 'jaws' in the head and draws blood and tissue fluids from its host. A cluster of the bright red worms can sometimes be seen protruding from the anus of a resting fish, notably in female Guppies. *Camallanus* produces thousands of tiny live larvae; these can be seen in faecal smears examined under a microscope. Apparent curvature of the spine can be suggestive of *Camallanus* infestation.

Trematodes – Intestinal flukes
The gill and skin flukes, such as *Dactylogyrus* and *Gyrodactylus*, are trematodes that are exterior parasites (so-called ectoparasites) of fishes and have only one host in their life cycles. The trematodes that live inside fishes (co-called endoparasites) usually have complex life cycles involving several hosts, such as water birds and snails, and the fish may be host to the adult or to one of the larval stages. The blood fluke *Sanguinicola*, for example, lives as an adult in the blood vessels of the gills in free-living Cyprinids, but seldom in aquarium

Below: *Typical life cycle of a digenetic trematode (with two or more hosts).*
1 *Eggs from adult flukes in water birds pass out in droppings.* 2 *Larvae infest water snails as an intermediate host.*
3 *Larvae from snail infest fish as second intermediate host.* 4 *Larvae ingested with fish develop into adult.*

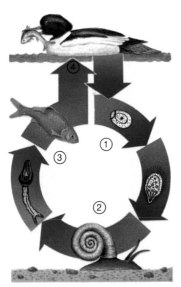

fishes. The eggs lodge in fine capillaries and can cause great damage in almost any organ of the body. Water snails act as the intermediate host in the life cycle. The trematode *Diplostomum*, on the other hand, reaches the adult stage in the intestine of water birds, but one larval stage in its cycle – the metacercaria – causes worm cataract in a fish's eye. Most mild infestations of trematodes, however, cause little distress to fishes.

Recommended treatments
Severe infestations of internal parasitic worms are difficult to cure. Certain veterinary products, such as praziquantel and levamisole, may be worth trying (see page 70-71).

Prevention is far more relevant than treatment in most cases, especially in those worms that have intermediate hosts that are easily removed.

LYMPHOCYSTIS – CAULIFLOWER OR RASPBERRY DISEASE
Signs of infection
Small white nodules appear on the skin and particularly on the fins. As they grow, they develop into cauliflower-shaped tumours up to 2mm (0.08in) across

Fishes affected
Lymphocystis can affect a wide variety of freshwater and marine species; Anabantids, such as Gouramies, seem to be particularly susceptible.

Details of infection
Lymphocystis is caused by a viral infection that can be transmitted from one fish to another. Sometimes it may be restricted to a few individuals; sometimes it may wipe out a whole community. In the early stages, the tumours can be mistaken for ich (see page 96), but the cauliflower-like appearance becomes obvious after several weeks. Eventually, infected fishes may waste away and die, or they may recover spontaneously.

Recommended treatment
As with all the viruses, treatment tends to be uncertain; opinions vary

Above: *A three-spot Gourami with signs of lymphocystis on the tail. The whitish nodules on the skin and fins are caused by a viral infection.*

Below: *Lymphocystis is affecting this Clubnosed Wrasse. The white growth near the base of the pectoral fin is a distinctive feature of the disease.*

on the prospect of a cure. Trimming the infected fins has been recommended, followed by painting with acrinol or triamcinolone acetonide. Using a bath containing a mixture of formalin and malachite green has been claimed to be successful, but this is unlikely. Since lymphocystis develops slowly, curing

it is likely to be a slow process. It may be wise to despatch affected fishes humanely and transfer any healthy fishes to a quarantine tank for at least two months. In the meantime, thoroughly disinfect the main aquarium (see page 64).

NEON DISEASE
(Pleistophora sp.)
See also false neon disease, described on page 88.
Signs of infection
As in many other diseases, erratic swimming behaviour is one of the first signs of infection. Emaciation may follow. The most characteristic symptom, however, is a spreading pale area within the muscles beneath the dorsal fin.

Fishes affected
This condition was originally found in Neon Tetras – hence the popular name of the disease. It is also known to attack other Characins and also some Cyprinids, such as Zebra Danios.

Details of infection
The causative organism, *Pleistophora hyphessobryconis*, is a sporozoan – a single-celled animal that reproduces by liberating millions of spores into the water. These spores are eaten with food and enter the intestine of healthy fishes. In the intestine or in the muscle, the spores turn into amoeba-like cells that spread throughout the body, forming groups of spherical cysts, particularly in the muscles. The cysts gradually replace the muscle fibres, and are released when the skin is damaged or when the fish dies. Infected fishes can therefore infect other fishes and themselves again and again.

Recommended treatment
No sure treatment has been found for this disease. There have been reports that modern anti-parasite treatments and those based on organic silver compounds are effective, but it is unlikely that heavily infected fishes can be saved.

It is worth trying to treat the water with peat (see photo on page 54) and using strong filtration with a diatom filter. The first thing to do is to remove any fishes with signs of the disease

Below: *These young Goldfishes have bulges in the region of the kidneys caused by the nodular disease sporozoan* Mitraspora cyprini.

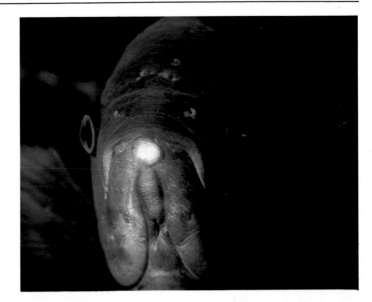

and then the only sure course of action is to strip down and completely disinfect the tank.

Above: *This Oscar exhibits a more obvious sign of nodular disease – a large swollen area harbouring the sporozoan parasites. Treatment is rarely effective in most cases.*

NODULAR DISEASES
(Myxobolus sp. and similar sporozoans)

Signs of infection
Infected fishes show rice-shaped cysts on the gills and skin, varying from pinhead-sized spots to boils as large as a pea and larger. Some species of *Myxobolus* form internal cysts, and related sporozoans may disrupt the balance mechanism of the fishes they infect; *Myxosoma cerebralis*, for example, causes so-called 'whirling disease' in Trout.

Fishes infected
This varied family of sporozoans affects many species of fish, particularly Cyprinids, but fortunately not too often in the aquarium. *Thélohanellus* (formerly *Myxobolus*) *piriformis* forms thread-like cysts on Tench and Weatherfish (*Misgurnus* sp.). *M. exiguus* causes pinhead-sized cysts on the skin of Carp.

Details of infection
Sporozoans are single-celled animals – literally 'spore animals' – that produce great quantities of spores as a means of reproduction and transmission from one fish to another. The life cycle varies according to species but broadly follows the same pattern. The spores are ingested by the fish and in the intestinal tract change into amoeba-like organisms that find their way into the bloodstream and lymphatic system. The organisms multiply and penetrate all the internal organs, eventually forming cysts internally and on the skin. When the external cysts rupture or a fish dies, millions of spores are released into the water, so starting a new cycle of infection.

Recommended treatment
Chemical remedies do not appear to be effective at any stage of the disease. It is best to destroy heavily infested fishes and to disinfect the tank or pond thoroughly (see page 64). Paradoxically, placing Glass Catfish with boil disease in clear, soft acid water with oak leaves is claimed to have been effective in clearing up the disease very quickly; perhaps altering the conditions in a similar way could pay dividends.

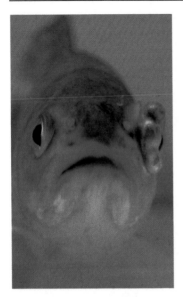

POP-EYE
(Exophthalmus)
Signs of infection
One or both eyes protrude abnormally. (Note: several fishes, particularly fancy Goldfishes, are bred with protruding eyes.)

Fishes affected
Pop-eye can affect a wide range of pond and aquarium fishes.

Details of infection
The progress and infectiousness of the disease depend very much upon the cause, which is often difficult to establish. Bulging eyes can result from a number of causes, including fish tuberculosis, ichthyosporidium, dropsy, worm cataract (caused by various larval trematodes such as *Diplostomum* sp.) and bacterial infections.

Above: *This head-on view clearly shows the bulging effect caused by pop-eye on one side of the fish.*

Recommended treatment
Using anti-parasite and anti-bacterial treatments may be effective.

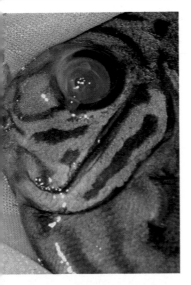

Above: *A combination of cloudy eye and pop-eye has afflicted this Discus, both bacterial infections.*

Left: *An Oscar with pop-eye caused by a TB infection behind it. The infection may have arisen from Goldfishes aready infected with TB given to it as food.*

Below: *This microphotograph of a skin scraping includes a specimen of* Gyrodactylus *sp. Inside its body the hooks of an embryo can be seen.*

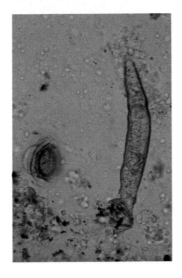

SKIN FLUKES
(Gyrodactylus sp.)
Signs of infection
Serious infections cause fishes to rub against hard objects, and the skin will appear opaque and possibly inflamed. Minor infections are unlikely to show any easily spotted symptoms.

Fishes affected
Most species of freshwater and marine fishes can become infected with *Gyrodactylus* and related species.

Details of infection
Skin flukes are trematode worms up to 0.8mm (0.03in) in length. They attach themselves to the skin (occasionally to the gills) by means of a sucker with two clasping hooks in the centre and feed on skin cells. It is possible to see the flukes clearly in a skin scraping viewed under a low-power microscope. *Gyrodactylus* is a monogenetic trematode, that is, the whole of the life cycle takes place on one host. The adult produces live young and, such as the vagaries of the parasitic life, that even the young worm has a younger worm developing within it, and this one has yet another within it, and so on.

Recommended treatment
A 3 percent salt dip will rid fishes of the parasites. Alternatively, use one of the modern anti-parasite remedies. It is possible to minimize infections by keeping fishes in clean conditions with good filtration. There are no resistant eggs, as in *Dactylogyrus* (see page 95).

SWIMBLADDER TROUBLE
Signs of trouble
Fishes are unable to maintain their position in the water: sometimes they cannot rise off the bottom without a great deal of effort; sometimes they cannot leave the top, and may even lie upside down at the surface.

Fishes affected
If the trouble is not caused by disease (refer to the diagnostic guide on page 75), then the problem may be due to malfunction of the swimbladder.

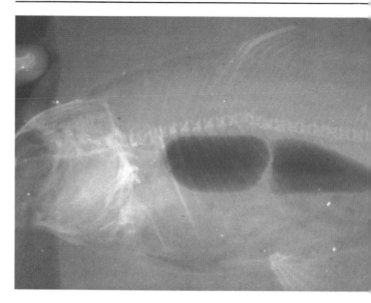

Above: *An X-ray of a Koi clearly reveals the shape and position of the swimbladder (and a fractured spine). Malfunction of the swimbladder can cause fishes buoyancy problems.*

Below: *A skin tumour is evident on this Goldfish. Often, cancerous growths are not visible and cause apparently unexplained deaths.*

Such problems are normally confined to deep-bodied fishes, particularly of the Carp family. Scaleless fishes also seem to be particularly susceptible.

Recommended treatment
There is no sure remedy for this condition. Since it is accelerated by cold water, a slight increase in temperature plus a mild salt bath can

often relieve the problem. Feeding Daphnia or worms can help by improving the digestion.

TUMOURS
Signs of trouble
Internal tumours can be detected only when they distend the body. External tumours show as projecting lumps on the affected fishes.

Above: *A Goldfish with a tumour on the head. Such problems can afflict any fish however well it is kept. Humane disposal is often needed. This is best achieved by putting the fish in a dish of ice cubes and putting this in a deep freeze.*

Fishes affected
Virtually any fish can be affected.

Details of condition
Tumours can be benign and confined to a given area, or they may be cancerous. Most tumours are incurable. Abnormal growth of the thyroid gland, which sometimes occurs, is occasionally curable.

Recommended treatment
Thyroid tumours need expert identification. They may be cured by prolonged baths in 5mg/litre of potassium iodide solution but, unless fish has a particular significance, it is usually advisable to dispose of it humanely (see page 74).

ULCER DISEASE
(Aeromonas sp., Pseudomonas sp. and others)
Signs of infection
Shallow, open sores, usually of a reddish colour, appear on the body and sometimes also on the fins.

Secondary infections, the most obvious of which is *Saprolegnia*, may set in. The lesions increase in size and merge as the disease progresses.

Above: *Large ulcers, as on this Goldfish, are generally caused by bacterial infection and lay the fishes open to secondary attack.*

Fishes affected
Coldwater Cyprinids are most commonly affected, particularly Goldfishes and Koi. This widespread disease has caused great losses in the commercial fish world.

Details of infection
The ulcers are caused principally by *Aeromonas* and *Pseudomonas* bacteria. The disease is highly contagious and can be spread by fishes, birds, nets etc. However, all fishes are not clinically affected; some may be carriers.

In Koi, different bacteria are commonly involved and the infection may be purely superficial. In Goldfishes, a chronic septicaemia often occurs, leading to dropsy and death.

Recommended treatment
Antibiotics in foods have been used, and the most promising approach so far is a specially prepared food that contains oxolinic acid. Proprietary treatments containing organic silver compounds are claimed to help; these may help the non-septicaemic

cases where the bacteria are just on the surface. Salt is a useful supportive treatment. Absolute cleanliness is essential; all equipment should be thoroughly sterilized. (For further details on how this should be carried out see page 64.)

VELVET DISEASE
(Oodinium pillularis)
Signs of infection
Fishes rub themselves against solid objects and may have difficulty in breathing. As the infection takes hold, a yellowish brown to greyish haze, intially made up of discrete dots, can be seen on the skin, which also becomes inflamed. Untreated fishes become emaciated. It is possible to see the individual parasites with a magnifying glass.

Fishes affected
Many freshwater species, particularly Anabantids and Cyprinids, may be affected. The parasites mainly colonize the skin but may also cause severe damage to the gills. Velvet often affects fry only a few days old, when it is quickly fatal.

Details of infection

The principal parasite involved, *Oodinium pillularis*, is a microscopic single-celled dinoflagellate, similar to *O. ocellatum* that causes coral fish disease in marine fishes. The individual organisms are pear-shaped and, in the parasitic stage, attach themselves to the outer skin of a fish by root-like growths. As the cells mature they fall away from the fish and develop into cysts on the aquarium floor. Inside the protective wall of the cyst each single cell divides repeatedly, forming up to 64 cells in four days, depending on the temperature. When the cyst breaks open, these cells are released and within a few minutes develop into free-swimming flagellated dinospores that seek a new host and become attached to the skin, so continuing the cycle of infection. If the dinospores fail to attach themselves to a fish within 24 hours, they die.

In common with many disease organisms, the parasites can keep a 'low profile' until conditions deteriorate. The cysts, for example, may not divide when they first form and lie dormant, but viable, for several months. Often, the only indication of *Oodinium* infection is the occasional unexplained death in the aquarium.

Recommended treatment

The various proprietary remedies available, most of which contain copper sulphate, are effective but should be used cautiously and exactly as the manufacturer recommends. Modern anti-parasite treatments are also worth trying. Both these types of remedy strike most effectively at the free-swimming dinospore stage of the parasitic cycle. Unfortunately, young fishes, which often show the symptoms first, are the most difficult to cure because they are so sensitive to the chemicals available for use in the aquarium.

Below: *The dotted haze on this Rasbora points to velvet disease. The dots are the single-celled parasites attached to the skin and fins.*

Additional Reading

Dr. H. R. Axelrod, Breeding Aquarium Fishes (6 volumes), TFH Publications

These volumes span 13 years from 1967, when the first volume was published, to 1980, when Volume 6 was published. The text contains much interesting information which will prove of great help in breeding many species of fishes. The fishes are dealt with individually. The style captures Dr. Axelrod's genuine enthusiasm for the subject. Superb pictures abound of breeding fishes.

Because the monographs on different fishes have been written as the information has become available, there is no particular sequential order between the books. All six volumes are really needed to provide a collection that will be treasured by any fishkeeper.

John Clegg, Freshwater Life, Frederick Warne and Co. Ltd.

A very readable and interesting book describing plants and invertebrate animals, with a short chapter on vertebrates. An authoritative standard reference book equally suitable for the expert and the beginner.

Dr. Mark Dulin, Diseases of Marine Aquarium Fishes, TFH Publications

Gives tips on maintaining the health of marine fishes, together with information on diseases.

Dr. Glenn L. Hoffman and Dr. Fred P. Meyer, Parasites of Freshwater Fishes, TFH Publications

A completely different book that lists treatments for many diseases. Does not contain diagnostic information.

Dr. George W. Post, Textbook of Fish Health, TFH Publications

An up-to-date book (1983) for the fishkeeper wanting to study the subject seriously. Biological knowledge is necessary to make full use of this book.

Dr. Karel Rataj and Thomas J. Horeman, Aquarium Plants, TFH Publications

This excellent and very readable book covers the identification, cultivation and ecology of coldwater and tropical freshwater plants.

Dr. H. Reichenback-Klinke, Fish Pathology, TFH Publications

An excellent book with many interesting details. A scientific knowledge, a level of dedication and a supply of dead fish are necessary to gain proper benefit.

Dr. Gottfried Schubert, Cure and Recognise Aquarium Fish Disease, TFH Publications

A useful little book for fishkeepers wishing to take their study one step further.

Dr. Lynwood S. Smith, Introduction to Fish Physiology, TFH Publications

Detailed and fascinating, but a scientific knowledge is needed to gain full benefit from the book.

Gunther Sterba, The Aquarists' Encyclopedia, Blandford Press

This incredible, fascinating book has information on all aspects of fishkeeping, including considerable detail on diseases. My choice for a desert island.

Dr. W. V. De Thabrew, Popular Tropical Aquarium Plants, Thornhill Press

An excellent book for fishkeepers wanting to grow a wide variety of tropical plants, giving in detail conditions required for each species. The illustrations vary in quality but this hardly detracts from the text.

Dr. W. V. De Thabrew, Coldwater Aquarium Plants, Thornhill Press

An invaluable book of similar quality to Dr. De Thabrew's tropical plant book.

Index

Page numbers in **bold** indicate major references, including accompanying photographs. Page numbers in *italics* indicate illustrations or charts. Text entries are shown in normal type.

A

Acanthocephala **100**
Achlya sp. **89-90**
Acid rain 13, 16
Acidity *see* pH
Acrinol *70-1*, 103
Aeration *30-1*, 56
Aeromonas sp. 71, **86-7, 109-10**
    hydrophila 89
    liquefaciens 89
Alkalinity *see* pH
Ammonia *16*, **25-8**
Amyloodinium ocellatum **84**
Anabantids 94, 102
Anchor worm 71, *75*, **78**, 83
Angelfishes 52, 63, 82, *88*, 89, 95, 96, 101
Aquascaping *44*, **50-2**
Argulus sp. **92-3**
    coregoni *93*
    foliaceus **93**
    japonicus **93**
Artemia salina 67

B

Bacterial septicaemias 92, **99**
Barbs *17*, 57, *63*, 82
Beacon fish 63
Benzalkonium chloride *70-1*, 83, 89
Bettas 64, 69
Black spot disease 71, *75*, **79-80**
Blood flagellates 71, *75*, **80**, 91
Bream 93
Breeding **48-57**
Bristle-nosed Catfish *56*

C

Calanus sp. **65**
Caligus sp. **65, 83**
    rapix **83**
Camallanus sp. **100-2**
Capillaria **101**
Carp 18, 57, 78, 79, 80, 86, 90, 93, 105, 108
Carp pox **93**
Catfishes *61*, 64, 101
Cauliflower disease **102-4**
Ceratophyllum sp. 43
Cestodes **100-1**
Characins *15*, *61*, 86, *88*, 94, 95, 104
Chilodonella **80-1**
Chilodonella sp. 71, *75*, **81**, 88
    cyprini **81**

Chloramphenicol *70-1*
Chloramine 25
Chlorine *24*, 25
Chondrococcus columnaris **82-3**
Cichlids *52, 53*, 55, 63, 78, 82, 96, 101
Ciliates 81, 86, 97
Clinostomum sp. 79
Cloudy eye *75*, **81**, 107
Clubnosed Wrasse *103*
Columnaris 71, *75*, **82-3**
Copepods *65*, 71, *75*, 78, **83-4**, 99
    with eggs *83*
Copper **24**
    compound 85, 86
Coral fish disease 56, 71, *75*, **84-5**, 111
Corydoras sp. 101
Costia 71, *75*, **85**
Cotton wool disease **82-3**
Cryptobia sp. *75*, **80**
    salmositica **80**
Cryptocaryon 71, 82, **85-6**
Cryptocaryon irritans **85-6**
Cyclops sp. *65*, 101
Cyprinids 78, 79, 80, 82, 94, 95, 104, 105, 110

D

Dace 79
Dactylogyrus sp. 71, **95**, 102, 107
Daphnia sp. *65*, **66**, *67*, 108
Dimetridazole *70-1*, 96
Dinoflagellates **84**, 111
Dinospore **84**, 111
Diplostomum sp. 102, 106
Discus 16, 27, *29, 52, 55*, 63, 81, 96, 101, *107*
    disease **96**
Doxycycline *70-1*
Dropsy *75*, **86-7**, 93, 106, 110
Duckweed 19

E

Egeria densa 19, 43
Eichhornia crassipes 52
Ergasilus sp. 71, *65*, **83-4**
    boettgeri **83**
    briani **83**
    minor **83**
    sieboldi **83-4**
    with eggs *83*
Exopthalmus **106**

F

False neon disease *71*, *75*, **88**
Festivum *53*
Filtration **31-9**, *54*, 98, 104
Fin-nipping 88-9, *89*
Finrot *75*, **88-9**
Fish fungus 84, **89-90**
Fish leech 67, *71*, **90-1**
Fish lice *71*, *75*, 83, **92-3**
Fish pox *75*, **93**
Fish tuberculosis *75*, 82, **94-5**, 106, *107*
Flagellae *71*, 90, 96
Flagellates 80, 85
Flexibacter columnaris **82**
Formaldehyde 74
Formalin 74, 95, 103
Fungal infection *90*
    spores *99*
    threads *71*
Fungi *71*, **89-90**
Fungus 57, **89-90**, 92

G

Gammarus sp. **66**, 100
    shrimps *66*
Giant Danios 64
Gill flukes 56-7, *71*, *75*, **95**
Glass Catfish 105
Glassfishes 95
Goldfishes 27, 54, 57, 63, 69, *78*, 79, 80, 82, *91*, *92*, 96, 97, *104*, *106*, *108-9*, *109*, 110
Gold-rimmed Tang *79*
Gouramies 51, 57, 64, 69, 96, 102
    Blue 68
    Dwarf 86, *94*
    Pearl *5*, 68
    Three-spot 95, *103*
Gyrodactylus sp. 102, **107**

H

Hardness *15*, **16-20**, 28
Hexamita sp. *71*, *75*, **96**
Hole-in-the-head **96**
Hydra sp. 45, 56, 66, **67-8**
Hyphae 89, 90

I

Ich/White spot 64, 74, *75*, 86, **96-8**
Ichthyobodo necator **85**
Ichthyophthirius 86, *98*, 102
    multifiliis **96-8**
Ichthyosporidium *71*, *75*, **98-9**, 106
    hoferi **98-9**
Inflammation *75*, **99**
Internal parasitic worms *71*, **100-2**
Intestinal flukes **102**
    worms *75*

Invertebrates 85, 86
Iron **24**

K

Koi 57, *82*, *84*, *87*, *93*, *108*, 110

L

Labeo bicolor 87
Labyrinth Fishes 56, 57, 64, 110
Leeches 45, *75*, 80 see also Fish leech
Lemna trisulca 19
Lernaea sp. 65, *78*, 83
    cyprinacaea **78**
    phoxinacaea **78**
Levamisole *70-1*, 102
Lighting 46-7, 54-6, *54*, 64-5
Livebearers 50, 54, 56, *61*, 74, 82, 86
Lymnaea ovata peregra 69
Lymphocystis *75*, **102-4**

M

Malachite green *70-1*, 90, 98, 103
Marshall Island Wrasse *94*
Melanoides tuberculata 69
Metacercaria 102
Methylene blue *34*, 56, *57*, *70-1*, 74, 90
Metronidazole *70-1*, 96
Minnows 78
Minocycline *70-1*
Misgurnus sp. 105
Mitraspora cyprini *104*
Moorish Idol 27
Mollies 82, 101
Mycelium 89
Mycobacterium sp. *71*, **94-5**
Myxobolus sp. **105**
    exiguus **105**
Myxosoma cerebralis 105

N

Nauplii 83, 84
Neascus cuticola **79-80**
Nematodes **101-2**
Neodiplostomum cuticola **79-80**
Neon disease *71*, *75*, **104**
Neons 63
Neon Tetra 16, 54, 104
Nifurpirinol *70-1*, 82, 83, 87, 88, 89
Nitrates *16*, *24-5*, 24-8, *26-7*
Nitrites *16*, 25-8, *26-7*
Nitrobacter sp. *26-7*, 27
Nitrogen cycle 25-28, *26-7*
Nitrosomonas sp. *26-7*, 27
Nocardia sp. **94-5**
Nodular diseases *75*, **104-5**

O

Octomitus sp. **96**
Oodinium sp. 24, 56, 82
    ocellatum **84-5**, 111
    pillularis 84, **110-1**
Orange Chromide 51
Ornamental Fish International (OFI) 58
Oscar *96, 105, 106*
Osmois **28-30**
Oxolinic acid *70-1*, 87, 110
Oxytetracycline *70-1*

P

Parachlorophenoxyethanol *70-1*, 87,
    89, 99
Parasitic worms *71*, **100-2**
pH **20-4**, *28*, 90
Phenoxyethanol 33, 56, *70-1*, 82, 83,
    89, 99
Pike 93
Piscicola geometra **90-1**
Planarians 56, **68-9**
Planorbis sp. *69*
Plants **40-7**, 50-2
Plastic plants 42-3, 62-3
Pleistophora sp. **104**
    hyphessobryconis 88, **104**
Pop-eye *75*, **106**, *107*
Posthodiplostomum cuticola **79**
Postassium iodide 109
    permanganate 78
Praziquantel *70-1*
Pseudomonas sp. **109-10**
    fluorescens **89**

R

Rainwater 15
Ramshorn snail *69*
Rasbora *111*
Raspberry disease **102-4**
Red Emperor *86*
Rift Valley Cichlids 63
Rosy Barbs 53, 57
Roundworms **101-2**

S

Salt *72-3*, 74, 81, 84, 85, 87, 90, 92,
    93, 95, 107, 108, 110
Salt water ich **85-6**
Sand snail 69
Sanguinicola sp. 102
Saprolegnia sp. *71, 75*, **89-90**, *91*,
    110
Siamese Fighting Fish *50*
Skin flukes *71, 75*, **107**
Skin papilloma **93**
Sleeping sickness **80**
Snails 45, 56, 69
Specific gravity 30, *30*

Spiny Boxfish *80-1*
Spironucleus sp. **96**
Sporozoans **104**, **105**
Swimbladder trouble *75*, **107-8**

T

Tailrot **88-9**
Tapeworms **100-1**
Tapwater 14-5
Tench 79, 80, 83, 86, 93, 105
Thélohanellus piriformis 105
Thorny headed worms **100**
Threadworms **101-2**
Thyroid gland 108
    tumour 108-9
Tomites *96*
Transportation **60,** *62*
Trematodes 95, **102**, 107
    larvae *71, 79*
Triamcinolone acetate *70-1*, 103
Triangle Cichlid *97*
Trichogaster leeri 5
Trypanoplasma sp. **80**
Trypanosoma sp. **80**, 91
Tubifex sp. 65, *66, 67*, 74, *100*, 101
Tumours *75*, **108-9**

U

Ulcer disease *75*, 86, 87, 89, **109-10**

V

Veiltails 89
Velvet disease 56, *71, 75*, 84, **110-1**
Vibrio anguillarium **89**

W

Wandering Snail 69
Waroo *97*
Water **12-39**
    cycle 12-14, *13*
    hardness 15, 16-20, 28
    natural sources 16
    pH 20-24, 28
    quality 53-4
    temperature 54
Water fleas *67*
Water hyacinths *44*, 52
Weatherfish 105
Whirling disease **104**
White Cloud Mountain Minnow 57
White spot/Ich 64, 74, *75*, 86, **96-8**
Worm cataract 102, 106

Y

Yellow grub *75*, 79

Z

Zebra Danios 52, 57, 104

Picture Credits

Artists
Copyright of the artwork illustrations on the pages following the artists' names is the property of Salamander Books Ltd.

Clifford and Wendy Meadway: 13, 38, 39, 83, 84, 85, 97, 99, 100, 102

Colin Newman (Linden Artists): 26-7, 29(T)

Photographs
The publishers wish to thank the following photographers who have supplied photographs for this book. The photographs have been credited by page number and position on the page: (B) Bottom, (T) Top, (C) Centre, (BL) Bottom left etc.

David Allison: Title page, 10-11, 20-1, 24-5(B), 32(B), 44(T), 50-1(B)

Chris Andrews (Tetra): 95, 108-9(B)

Eric Crichton © Salamander Books Ltd: 17(T), 18, 19, 22, 23, 24(T), 28, 30, 31, 32(T), 33(BR), 34, 35, 36(B), 37(C), 39(T), 42(B), 43, 54(BL)

David Ford: 90, 99(B), 106(T), 109(T), 110

Jan-Eric Larsson: 37(B), 40-1, 48-9, 52, 55, 58-9, 64-5, 66(B), 68(T,B), 69, 76-7, 88-9(B), 91(T), 98, 100-1(T), 111

Dick Mills: 16-17(B), 33(BL), 45(T), 53(C,B), 57(T), 62(T)

Laurence Perkins: 92(T)

Bernard Pye: 44(B), 54(BR)

Rod Roberts: 60

Mike Sandford: Half-title page, 15(B), 42(T), 46-7, 51(T), 56(T,C), 62-3(B), 66(T), 67, 87(B), 92(B)

David Sands: Endpapers, copyright page, 12, 14-5(T), 29(B), 57(B), 61, 79(B), 80-1(B), 86, 88(B), 91(B), 94(T,B), 96(TR), 97(B), 103(T,B), 105, 107(T)

Peter W. Scott: 78, 79(T), 81(T), 82, 84(T), 87(T), 93(T), 96(TL), 104, 106(B), 107(B), 108(BL)

Acknowledgements
The publishers wish to thank the following companies and individuals for their assistance in preparing this book: Algarde; Aquamagic Ltd.; Aquarian Laboratories; Aquarium Systems Inc.; Hockney Engineers Ltd.; Interpret Ltd.; Tetra Fish Care; Dr. Christopher Andrews; Mrs. Sue Chick; Dr. David Ford; Mr. David Sands; Mr. M. A. Smith Evans; Dr. Vivian De Thabrew.